FIELD&
STREAM

THE ESSENTIAL
FISHING
HANDBOOK

JOE CERMELE
and the editors of *Field and Stream*

weldon**owen**

CONTENTS

TOOLS

CONTENTS

TECHNIQUES

CONTENTS

TACTICS

FISHING IS JOYOUSLY SIMPLE

and fascinatingly complex. If hooking a panfish on a worm under a bobber doesn't make you smile, you should go see a doctor. You can also spend your whole life trying to master surf casting for striped bass, and no matter how proficient you become, there will always be more for you learn. The key to becoming a truly great angler is to recognize that the two ends of the spectrum are not mutually exclusive. If you pursue both with the same zeal, the sport of fishing can make it easy for you to avoid boredom throughout your whole life. That's the goal of this book. The tactics, tips, tackle, and technique give you the tools. It's up to you to go out on the water and find your fun. Go for it.

TOOLS

IT'S HAPPENED A THOUSAND TIMES.

A non-angler walks into my garage, looks around, and says: "Do you really need that many rods to catch fish?" I always answer that question with another question: "Do you play 18 holes of golf with nothing but a putter?" There is no one rod, reel, bait, or lure that will get the job done in every situation. This chapter gives you a solid foundation in which tackle, baits, lures, and flies are necessary for a wide variety of fishing situations. It also helps you better understand how these elements function for angling success, so you know what you need—and why—when you walk into the tackle shop. You'll also get tips on maintenance because keeping tackle well-tuned is as important as changing the oil in your car.

1 USE THE ALL-TIME 15 GREATEST LURES

Whether you target bass or walleyes, trout or stripers, salt- or freshwater fish, these lures work. Some your granddad fished. Others have earned a reputation for productivity in more recent decades. In any case, these catch fish, time after time.

MANN'S 1-MINUS This crankbait easily skims the top of barely submerged weedbeds. That's often where the bass live.

CURLY TAIL GRUB Combined with a plain or painted roundhead jig, these are arguably the most versatile fishing lures of all time.

RAPALA ORIGINAL FLOATER Loved by trout, bass, walleyes, and pike alike. Size F11 is great for all species, and black over silver is a top color.

PANTHER MARTIN A staple from Montana to Maine, these spinners are perfect for picking trout from the pockets of steeply tumbling mountain creeks.

KASTMASTER Great for its lively, tight wobble on a fairly fast retrieve and a broad shape that resembles a small freshwater shad.

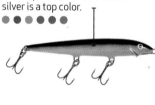

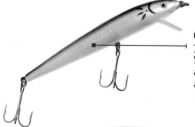

CORDELL RED FIN The 7-inch, 1-ounce (18 cm, 28 g) Smoky Joe–color Red Fin is a striper killer in both fresh and saltwater.

REBEL POP-R There are lots of poppers on the market, but this one casts farther than most and spits water like no other.

KEY

- BASS
- TROUT
- WALLEYE
- PANFISH
- PIKE/ MUSKIE
- SALMON/ STEELHEAD
- SALTWATER

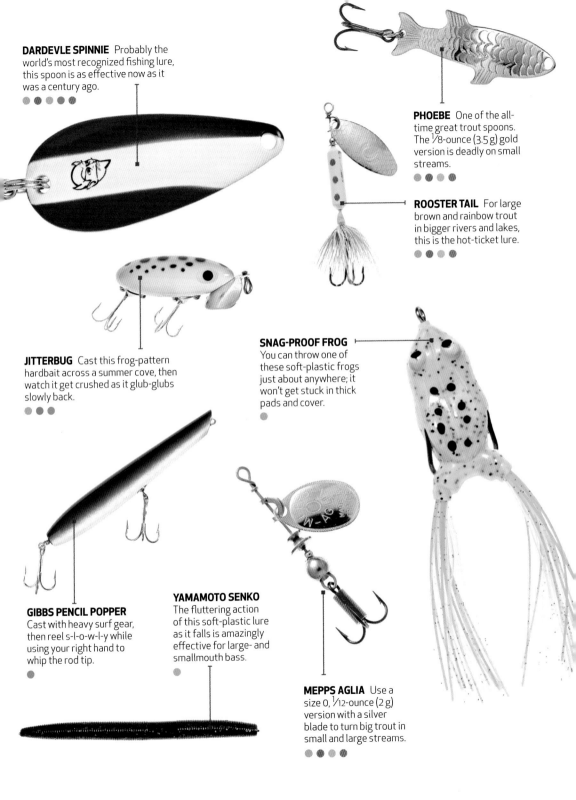

DARDEVLE SPINNIE Probably the world's most recognized fishing lure, this spoon is as effective now as it was a century ago.

PHOEBE One of the all-time great trout spoons. The 1/8-ounce (3.5 g) gold version is deadly on small streams.

ROOSTER TAIL For large brown and rainbow trout in bigger rivers and lakes, this is the hot-ticket lure.

JITTERBUG Cast this frog-pattern hardbait across a summer cove, then watch it get crushed as it glub-glubs slowly back.

SNAG-PROOF FROG You can throw one of these soft-plastic frogs just about anywhere; it won't get stuck in thick pads and cover.

GIBBS PENCIL POPPER Cast with heavy surf gear, then reel s-l-o-w-l-y while using your right hand to whip the rod tip.

YAMAMOTO SENKO The fluttering action of this soft-plastic lure as it falls is amazingly effective for large- and smallmouth bass.

MEPPS AGLIA Use a size 0, 1/12-ounce (2 g) version with a silver blade to turn big trout in small and large streams.

2 MEET 15 NEW CLASSICS

These crankbaits, soft plastics, and jigs—plus some in categories all their own—are the hottest baits on bass impoundments, walleye lakes, and trout streams today because they catch fish consistently. Better start making room in your tackle box.

SPRO PRIME BUCKTAIL Not all bucktails are created equally. The head shape and eye position of the Spro gives it a flutter that's unmatched.

MUSKY INNOVATIONS BULL DAWG Its nose-down falling orientation and high-vibration tail turn trophy-muskie heads.

ZOOM FLUKE The Fluke is at its best when rigged weedless and worked in a twitch-fall pattern off the bottom.

RAPALA X-RAP Works best when twitched aggressively, producing an irresistible side-to-side slashing action.

GULP! MINNOW If a fish eats baitfish, it'll eat a Gulp! Minnow. This versatile soft bait comes in a range of sizes.

MANN'S STRETCH 25+ These lures dive up to 30 feet (9 m) deep unassisted when trolled, making them staples on saltwater boats.

KEY

- BASS
- TROUT
- WALLEYE
- PANFISH
- PIKE/ MUSKIE
- SALMON/ STEELHEAD
- SALTWATER

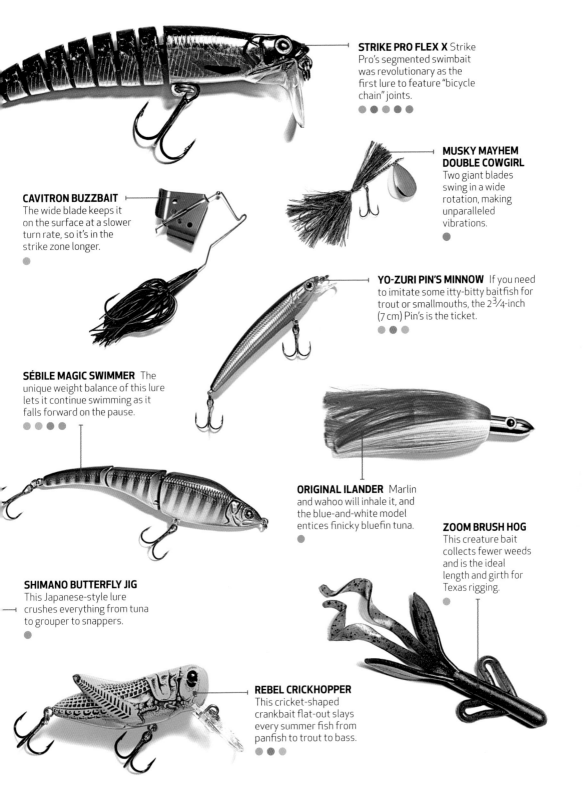

STRIKE PRO FLEX X Strike Pro's segmented swimbait was revolutionary as the first lure to feature "bicycle chain" joints.

MUSKY MAYHEM DOUBLE COWGIRL Two giant blades swing in a wide rotation, making unparalleled vibrations.

CAVITRON BUZZBAIT The wide blade keeps it on the surface at a slower turn rate, so it's in the strike zone longer.

YO-ZURI PIN'S MINNOW If you need to imitate some itty-bitty baitfish for trout or smallmouths, the 2¾-inch (7 cm) Pin's is the ticket.

SÉBILE MAGIC SWIMMER The unique weight balance of this lure lets it continue swimming as it falls forward on the pause.

ORIGINAL ILANDER Marlin and wahoo will inhale it, and the blue-and-white model entices finicky bluefin tuna.

ZOOM BRUSH HOG This creature bait collects fewer weeds and is the ideal length and girth for Texas rigging.

SHIMANO BUTTERFLY JIG This Japanese-style lure crushes everything from tuna to grouper to snappers.

REBEL CRICKHOPPER This cricket-shaped crankbait flat-out slays every summer fish from panfish to trout to bass.

3 RIG ME SOFTLY

These four rigging methods will get any style of soft-plastic lure ready for action.

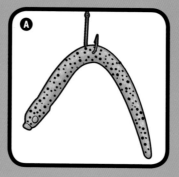

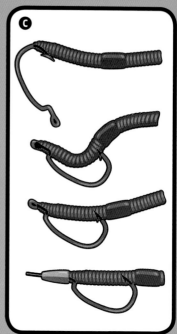

WACKY RIG (A) This killer setup for bass involves hooking slim soft-plastic bait through the middle. Both ends are left free to wiggle, and in most cases no weight is added. It's especially effective with Senkos.

TUBE RIG (B) There are several good ways to rig tubes such as the Gitzit. Most often I go with a small internal jighead. For a 3½-inch (9 cm) tube, use a 2/0 ⅜-ounce (10.5 g), insider-style jighead. Insert the hook in the tube's head and rotate it so it passes down inside the body without exiting. Continue by forcing the head of the jig into the tube, leaving only the hook eye exposed. Then work the hook point out and through the tube at the rear so the tube lies straight.

CAROLINA RIG (C) To make this common rig for bottom dredging, Texas-rig a worm or lizard but leave the hook eye exposed. Tie 18 inches (46 cm) of clear leader between the hook and a small barrel swivel. On your main line, thread a brass Carolina weight (or lead sinker), followed by a small red glass bead, and tie your main line to the other side of the swivel. The weight will click against the glass bead as you fish to help attract bass.

TEXAS RIG (D) Most often used with plastic worms and lizards, this rig is adaptable to other baits, like jerkbaits. Put a conical worm weight on the line first and then attach the hook. Thread the hook point about ½ inch (1.25 cm) into the worm's head and then through the worm's underside. Slide the worm up the hook shank so it just covers the hook eye. Rotate the hook until it faces upward toward the worm's body. Grab the worm right behind the hook bend, push its body slightly forward, and then bring it back down on the hook point until

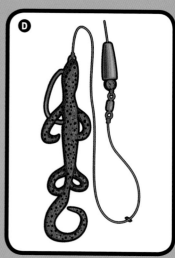

the point is almost but not quite all the way through the plastic. The bait should now lie straight. I use a 3/0 Gamakatsu offset-shank worm hook for a typical 6- or 7-inch (15 to 18 cm) worm, but any similar style is fine.

4 FISH THE TOP 10 FRESHWATER BAITS

Not sure what to buy at the tackle shop? You can't go wrong with one of these.

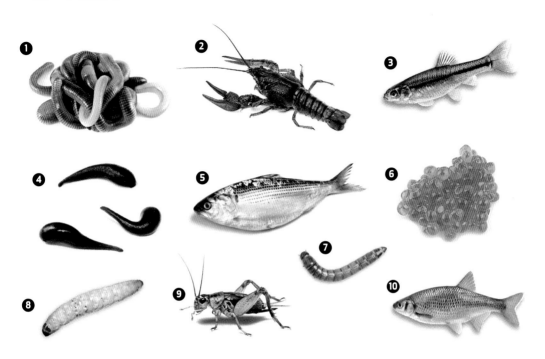

1. NIGHTCRAWLERS Whether you dig your own or pick up a container at the tackle shop, nightcrawlers are arguably the most universal bait used in freshwater.

2. CRAYFISH These freshwater crustaceans, best fished in rocky areas, are candy to bass, walleyes, and perch. You can use a whole live crayfish or just the tail meat.

3. FATHEAD MINNOWS These small, relatively inexpensive baitfish can be fished by themselves on a plain hook or on lead jighead for deeper presentations, as in ice fishing.

4. LEECHES Their dark color stands out in the water, and their wiggle is hard for fish to resist. They'll catch everything from perch to smallmouths but are best known as the premier live bait for walleyes.

5. GIZZARD SHAD A live adult gizzard shad makes an excellent bait for trophy freshwater striped bass, pike, muskies, and even blue and flathead catfish.

6. SALMON EGGS Although these salmon eggs won't catch a wide variety of species, if you're after members of the trout family, they are quite tempting.

7. MEALWORMS Available in orange and red colorations, these beetle larvae have an armor-like exterior that makes them hearty, and their bright color helps them stand out in the water.

8. WAXWORMS The caterpillar larvae of wax moths, waxworms are very tiny but very potent. They'll catch trout anywhere they live, but "waxies" shine as panfish baits.

9. CRICKETS These insects are delicate and don't live long on the hook, but then it doesn't take long for a bluegill, trout, or crappie to slurp one up. Find them at a bait or pet shop.

10. SHINERS "Shiner" is used to refer to any silver- or gold-scaled baitfish species. Use large golden shiners for largemouth bass or pike, smaller ones for trout, crappies, and smallies.

5 PICK THE BEST REEL FOR THE JOB

Anglers love to debate spinning vs. baitcasting reels. It's not that one is better—it's that spinning and baitcasting are two very different things. Spinning in freshwater usually means lighter line and lighter lures—usually 12-pound (5.4 kg) test or less. Baitcasting is done with heavier line and lures. Experienced anglers use both, depending on the circumstances. Going for a big brute of a muskie? Baitcasting is probably your best bet. Jigging for perch in a river? Try a spinning outfit.

BAITCASTING REEL The spool on a baitcasting reel revolves on an axle as it pays out line. By applying thumb pressure to the revolving spool, an angler can slow and stop a cast with pinpoint precision. Baitcasting reels require skill and practice and are a favorite of bass anglers, many of whom insist the reels afford more sensitive contact with the line than spinning reels. Baitcasters get the nod from trolling fishermen, because the revolving spool makes it easy to pay out and take up line behind a boat and also reduces line twist.

LEVEL-WIND GUIDE Attached to a worm gear, this device evenly moves the line back and forth across the face of the spool to prevent line from getting trapped under itself.

SPOOL Holds the fishing line.

STAR DRAG Adjusts tension on a stacked series of washers and brake linings that make up the reel's internal drag.

SPOOL TENSIONER A braking device to reduce spool overrun and resultant "bird's nests" line snarls.

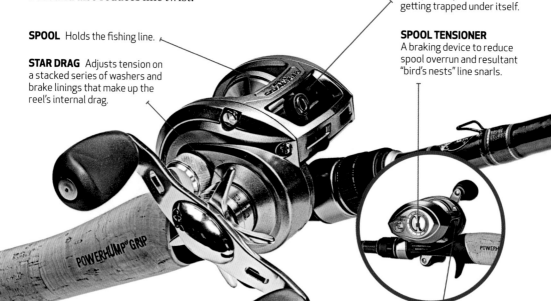

HANDLE The latest upgrades offer ergonomic grips with grooves for better control.

FREESPOOL BUTTON Allows the spool to turn freely for the cast.

REEL FOOT Slides into mounting slots of the rod's reel seat.

SPOOL Holds the fishing line. A skirted spool covers the main reel shaft like a skirt to prevent line entanglement.

BAIL Serves as a line pickup device to return the line evenly on the spool after the cast.

GEAR HOUSING Protects the internal gears that connect the handle to the spool.

DRAG ADJUSTMENT KNOB The drag is a system of friction washers and discs. Front-mounted drags are typically stronger than rear-mounted drags.

ANTI-REVERSE LEVER Prevents the reel handle from turning as line is paying out.

SPINNING REEL Spinning reels have fixed spools that do not rotate—the line uncoils from the front of the spool, pulled by the weight of the lure. Since the cast lure doesn't need to have enough force to spin a rotating spool, spinning reels can utilize very light lures—ultralight spinning reels can handle lures as feathery as $1/32$ of an ounce (1 g)—and backlash is rarely an issue. The downside to spinning reels: Stopping a cast isn't a straightforward task. And spinning reels are notorious for twisting line. It's best to pump the rod up, then reel on the way down to minimize twist.

HANDLE Activates the gears to retrieve line. Spinning reels come in a wide range of gear ratios, which is the number of spool revolutions to the number of gear handle revolutions. High-speed retrieve reels have gear ratios in the 4:1 class or higher. Lower gear ratios support more cranking power.

6 GET SOME GUIDANCE

All fishing rods start out blank. Some are weighted and tapered for making fly rods, while others are designed to be the base for big-game saltwater rods that can battle a marlin. What really makes a rod function properly are the guides. Understand how guides work, and you'll understand why different rod styles are better suited to varying fishing situations. These guide styles and configurations are the ones you're most often going to find in your local tackle shop.

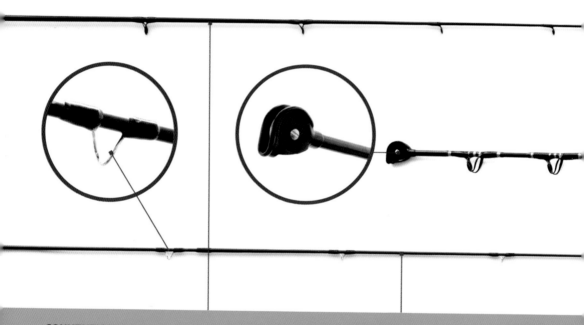

CONVENTIONAL ROD Conventional and bait-casting reels sit on the top side of the rod, and reel line straight onto a narrow spool. They're not as wide as spinning reel guides, and they generally taper very quickly to a small-diameter tip guide. Line comes off these reels very quickly, so it's important that it stays channeled to achieve maximum accuracy and distance. Some companies now make conventional rods with super-tiny "micro guides" all along the blank. It's believed that the smaller the guides, the more accurate the cast, especially when used with the ultra-thin braided lines and super lines popular today. The small diameter and fast taper of conventional guides also aid in accuracy in short, delicate presentations with methods like flipping, which are much harder to achieve with a spinning rod.

FLY ROD With the exception of the first guide on a fly rod—which is wider and thicker and known as the stripping guide—fly rods are built with light thin-wire guides, often called "snake guides." Since the reel never comes into play in terms of cast distance or accuracy, snake guides are designed to simply let the fly line pass through freely and without obstruction while adding as little weight to the rod as possible. To that end, it's important to always make sure snake guides are aligned properly and don't have any grit or residue buildup on the inside. You want the guides to remain as smooth as possible to maximize your casting distance and accuracy. The stripping guide is wider and beefier because it takes the most strain when stripping streamer flies. You'll often find two stripping guides on heavier fly rods used for saltwater fishing.

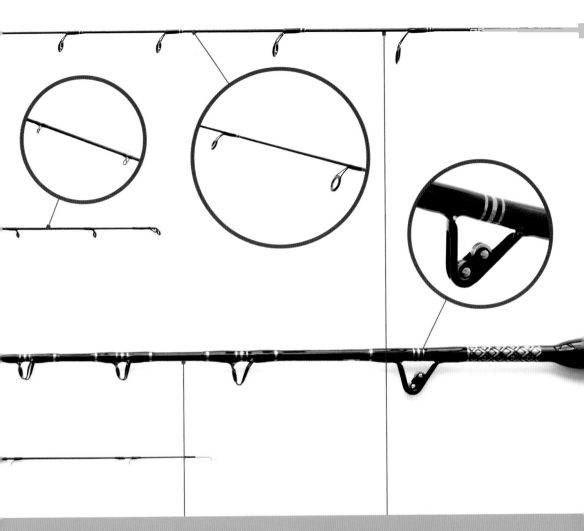

BIG-GAME ROD Uniquely designed for the rods that stand up to tuna, marlin, and swordfish, roller guides have heavy-duty metal frames and feature one or two smooth wheels on bearings that turn freely within the frame. Big-game rods with roller guides are not meant to be cast, but are almost exclusively used for trolling. The bearings up the chances that the thick-diameter monofilament line typically used for big-game pursuits won't catch or snag in the heat of the moment, but, more important, they ensure that line flows through the guides as smoothly as possible when a fish grabs a lure on the troll and starts peeling drag. Some rods designed for jigging may feature a roller guide at the tip or as the first guide closest to the reel, but if you're looking for versatility in a saltwater rod, you'll likely want to skip the rollers.

SPINNING ROD Spinning rod guides taper more drastically than those on any other rod. Because spinning reels have wider spools and retrieve line in wide loops, the first guide closest to the reel is often referred to as the gathering guide. This guide is the widest in diameter on the rod, which both allows line being retrieved to wind on the spool evenly and doesn't constrict line coming off the reel during the cast. This helps achieve smoother, longer casts. Make sure your spinning reel is the proper size for the rod you're using. If it's too big, the gathering guide may not be wide enough to wind the line properly, causing loops and tangles in your spool. Many anglers prefer spinning rods with 7 to 8 guides or more, because the more guides, the greater the taper as the line passes through, and the more accurate the cast.

7 PERFORM EMERGENCY GUIDE REPAIRS

A broken guide shouldn't be the end of a perfectly fine rod, or a great fishing trip. For strength, durability, and speed, nothing beats a strip of shrink-wrap to attach a new guide. In the fall, local marinas or boatyards have scraps from winterizing that you can pick up for free, and you can buy an assortment of guides at local tackle shops. Make a repair kit and keep it in your boat.

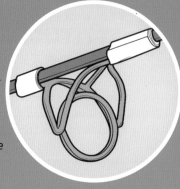

STEP 1 Cut a triangular piece of shrink-wrap long enough to wrap three times around your rod. The width of the base should extend beyond the foot of the guide.

STEP 2 Cut off the threads and foot of the broken guide with a razor.

STEP 3 Select the appropriate-size guide replacement.

STEP 4 Tape the new guide to the rod blank.

STEP 5 Wrap 1 foot (30.5 cm) with shrink-wrap.

STEP 6 Heat with a lighter, but be careful not to get the flame too close or you risk melting the shrink-wrap.

STEP Repeat steps 1 through 6 on the second guide foot.

8 LET THE ROD DO THE WORK

Spinfishermen and baitcasters can throw a line with greater distance and accuracy by leaving half a rod's length of line hanging from the rod tip when casting. This extra length causes the rod tip to flex deeper when the cast is made, generating more power from the rod with less effort from the wrist and arm. The reduced physical exertion permits better hand-eye coordination.

9 HAVE A CANE-DO ATTITUDE

You could use one of those fancy side-scan sonar depthfinders with the new underwater fish-eye orthographic readouts. Or you could go cut a switch of bamboo and do a little cane-pole fishing. If you choose the latter, a decent cane pole is as close as the nearest stand of bamboo. Ordinary backyard bamboo works just fine for panfish, bass, and small catfish. Make a cane pole our way, with the line anchored to the pole along its entire length, and you'll be able to land anything that doesn't pull you into the pond first.

STEP 1 Start by cutting yourself a straight piece of cane about 10 feet (3 m) long. Next, trim the leaf stems as close as possible. Saw through the fat end at the bottom of a joint so the butt end will have a closed cap. Finally, smooth the rough edges with sandpaper.

STEP 2 Tie a string to the slender tip. Suspend the cane as it dries to tan color (could take several weeks). Straighten a curved pole by weighting it with a brick.

STEP 3 Using an arbor knot, attach 20-pound (9 kg) line a few inches above where you hold the rod. Lay the line along the length of the pole and whip-finish the running line to the rod with old fly line at two spots—a few feet apart—in the middle of the rod and at the tip. (You do this so if the rod tip breaks, the line will remain attached to the pole.) Attach a 2-foot (60 cm) monofilament leader. Total length of line from tip of rod should be 14 to 16 feet (4 to 5 m). Finish with a slip bobber, split shot, and a long-shank hook.

10 KNOW YOUR BLUEGILL

Most anglers cut their teeth as kids chasing these easy-to-catch scrappers at the neighborhood pond or creek. Bluegills will eat anything from a fresh, lively cricket to a ball of stale white bread on a hook. Don't want to use bait? Any little fly, small spinner, soft-plastic grub jig, or tiny crankbait will do. But these aggressive fish aren't all child's play; serious grown-up anglers invest a lot of time hunting the biggest of the big in lakes and reservoirs across the country, as bluegills can break 2 pounds and are excellent on the table. The current world-record bluegill weighed in at an amazing 4 pounds, 12 ounces (2 kg). If it's jumbo fish you're after, search around weedbeds, humps, and brush piles in 5 to 10 feet (1.5 to 3 m) of water. If you just want to catch a whole mess and don't care about size, find the local public dock, cast a worm under a bobber, and start having fun.

11 PUT ON THE BRAKES

When it comes to setting the drag, lots of fishermen don't have a clue. The general rule for monofilament lines is that drag setting should be about one-third of the line's breaking strength. Say you're fishing with 12-pound-test (5.5 kg) mono. That means you should tighten your reel's drag until it takes 4 pounds (1.8 kg) of force to take line from the reel. Play with a drag knob and tug on the line while guessing at the setting, but it's far better to actually measure it. Try a simple 20-pound (9 kg) spring scale hooked to a line loop at the reel.

There are times when you need a tighter drag setting, but that applies only to comparatively heavy tackle. Some hardcore bass anglers lock down their drags when fishing thick cover—both to get a solid hookset and to haul big fish out of the weeds. In testing different freshwater baitcasting reels by tightening the star-drag knobs as hard as possible by hand, I found that they actually don't lock down at all. I could pull line from the reel in most cases with 8 to 10 (3.5 to 4.5 kg) pounds of force. With lighter lines, back off the drag a bit or risk disaster. Also, be sure to set drag based not on the line strength alone, but on the weakest link between the reel and your lure or bait, such as a knot.

12 UNRAVEL BACKLASHED LINE

Make an excellent tool for unraveling backlashes from a No. 2 fishing hook. Using pliers, straighten the hook and flatten the barb. Then use a file to dull the point slightly. Push the eye of the hook deep into a wine cork and glue it in place. Use this cork-handled tool to pick loops of line out of the tangle until it clears.

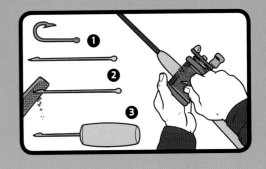

13 OVERHAUL YOUR REEL IN 15 MINUTES

Think of your reel like your car engine. Run it hard year after year without proper maintenance, and it won't be long before it seizes. This quick procedure is like an oil change for your baitcaster or spinning reel. Do it before the season, and you'll crank in fish all summer long.

STEP 1 Remove your old line (even if it's new) and recycle it.

STEP 2 Unscrew the drag cap and remove the spool. Then take off the handle cap and unscrew the winding handle in a clockwise direction. Lay out all of the parts on a clean work space in the same order in which you dismantled them for easy reassembly.

STEP 3 Rinse the entire reel with hot water to remove any sand or grit. Once it's completely dry, spray a nonflammable solvent (gun solvents work well) on metal parts to remove dirty grease and oil. Let it dry, then wipe the reel with a clean cloth.

STEP 4 Put one drop of oil each in all of the holes, as well as on the shaft and any exposed bearings. Then dab threaded surfaces and gears with grease. Only apply reel-approved products. Don't use WD-40, which leaves a hard-to-remove finish when heated. Less is best with oil and grease. Extra lubricant can slow the reel down. Reassemble it all, spool new line, and go fishing.

14 CHOOSE THE RIGHT LINE

CHARACTERISTIC	NYLON	VS	FLUOROCARBON	ADVANTAGE
LONGEVITY	Deteriorates in UV light (sunlight)		Not affected by UV	Fluorocarbon lasts longer
WATER ABSORPTION	Absorbs water and weakens slightly		Does not absorb water	Fluorocarbon is stronger when wet
DENSITY	Close to that of water		About 60% denser than nylon; sinks readily	Nylon can be made to float or sink in fishing
COLD WEATHER	Becomes stiffer		Unaffected by temperature extremes	Fluorocarbon is a good ice-fishing line
KNOT STRENGTH	Moderate to high		Moderate to high	A draw; depends on knot type
ABRASION RESISTANCE	Moderate to low		High	Fluorocarbon is best in heavy cover
PRICE	Low to moderate		High	Nylon is more affordable

15 LEAD THE WAY

In most circumstances, clear fluorocarbon line is less visible to fish than nylon monofilament of the same size. (It is not completely invisible underwater despite what you might have heard.) If you're after leader-shy fish such as winter steelhead in low, clear water or sharp-eyed false albacore in the salt, using fluorocarbon line makes perfect sense. Some kind of low-visibility fluorocarbon leader is also a good idea for trout, bass, and other fish made wary by fishing pressure. Abrasion resistance is also a huge plus. When these lines get nicked or scratched from being dragged across structure by a heavy fish, they are much less likely to break than comparable nylons. You have lots of knot options for making

leaders. I usually use a four-turn surgeon's knot to attach a fluorocarbon fly-fishing tippet, for example, and back-to-back Uni knots with heavier lines.

16 TIE A PALOMAR KNOT

This is the most widely useful—and the easiest "to tie—of all terminal knots that you'll see used in freshwater and inshore saltwater fishing. It works well with both nylon monofilaments and superbraids, and will soon be your new best friend in the knot world.

STEP 1 Extend about 6 inches (15 cm) of doubled line through the eye of the hook or lure.

STEP 2 Tie a loose overhand knot using the doubled line on either side of the eye. The hook itself will hang from the middle of the knot.

STEP 3 Pass the loop over the hook. Wet the knot with saliva and then pull on the doubled line (but not the loop) to tighten. Trim closely.

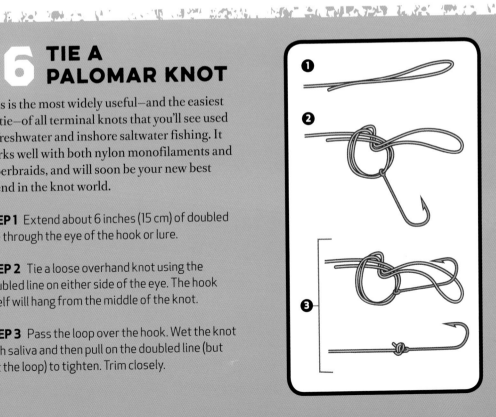

17 GET INTO HEAVY METAL

BULLET SINKER

MODELS: Lead, brass, steel, or tungsten; painted, free-sliding, or self-pegging.

USES: Casting or pitching Texas-rigged soft plastics.

RIGGING: Run the line through the sinker's pointed end and tie it to a worm hook.

TIPS: Use the lightest sinker needed to maintain bottom contact or to penetrate cover. Let the sinker slide free for open water; peg the sinker to the head of the bait amid thick cover.

EGG SINKER

MODELS: Lead, steel, or bismuth.

USES: Carolina-rigging soft-plastic bass lures; drifting and bottom-fishing live bait for everything from trout to stripers.

RIGGING: Run line through the sinker and tie it to a two-way swivel. Attach a leader and hook to the other side.

TIPS: This allows a fish to run with the bait without feeling its weight. Over a snag-filled bottom, pinch a split shot on the line in place of the swivel.

DROP SINKER

MODELS: Lead, steel, or tungsten; round, teardrop, or cylindrical.

USES: Fishing small soft plastics in deep water.

RIGGING: Tie a drop-shot hook to the line with a Palomar knot, leaving a long tag line to attach the sinker.

TIPS: After the sinker touches down, gently pull the line taut without moving the sinker. Then drop the rod tip and let the lure free-fall slowly to the bottom.

WALKING SINKER

MODELS: Lead or steel; Lindy-style or banana-shape (bottom weighted).

USES: Presenting live bait to walleyes. They're either dragged over the bottom behind a drifting boat or trolled.

RIGGING: Thread the line through a walking sinker and tie it to a swivel. To the other side, tie a 3- to 6-foot (1 to 3 m) 6-pound-test (3 kg) leader with a live-bait hook.

TIPS: Banana-type models are more resistant to snags.

PINCH-ON SINKER

MODELS: Lead or tin; round, clam, bullet, or elongated.

USES: Getting lures, flies, and bait deeper in the water for trout, bass, catfish, and other species. They're most often used in stream and river fishing.

RIGGING: Pinch the shot or sinker to the line above the hook or lure.

TIPS: Pinch-on weights are best used for casting. The clam and bullet shapes are more snag resistant.

18 ADJUST YOUR BOBBER TO THE FISH

BLUEGILLS When bluegills are on or near spawning beds in early spring, set your bobber to fish shallow with only 2 or 3 feet (.6 to .9 m) of line, holding your bait a few inches off the bottom. Later in summer, when bigger bluegills have moved to offshore bottom humps 10 to 12 feet (3 to 3.5 m) deep, slide your bobber stop up the line to fish the same terminal gear at those depths.

TROUT For both resident stream trout and steelhead, adapt the tactic to moving water. To work a run of moderate current that's 4 feet (1.25 m) deep, set your bobber so the worm, salmon egg, or small jig is just above the bottom as the bobber drifts with the current. Cast up and across the stream, then hold your rod high; keep as much slack line as possible out of the current to avoid drag on the bobber while following the drift with your rod. When the bobber pauses or darts underwater, set the hook.

WALLEYES Put a wriggly leech on a size 6 or 8 hook, add some small split shots, and set your slip bobber to fish at the same depth as the outside edge of a deep weedline. Ideally, a light breeze will drift both your boat and the floating bobber slowly along the edges of the vegetation, so you'll cover lots of water with very little effort.

BASS Set your slip bobber shallow to fish a frisky 3-inch (7.5 cm) live shiner along shoreline structure. When you come to some deeper structure off a shoreline point, it takes only a few seconds to adjust your bobber stop and fish the same shiner 10 feet (3 m) deeper and right on the money.

19 CHANGE HOOKS FOR BETTER FISHING

Remove those treble hooks from your lures and replace them with straight-shank hooks one size larger. Attach the single hook to the lure's forward hook mount and leave the rear bare. Fish often hit lures headfirst, so you will get just as many hookups, and the release will be easier.

20 PLAY THE BAITING GAME

After you've made the effort to catch fresh live bait (or buy it from a gas-station vending machine), having it constantly fall off the hook can lead to a short, aggravating day of fishing. Be sure to rig your bait on the correct-style hook.

	CIRCLE	LIGHT WIRE RING	ABERDEEN	BAIT-HOLDER	KAHLE
BASICS	Turned-in point impales fish in the corner of the mouth.	The ring on this hook lets baitfish swim freely.	Encourages bites and penetrates easily.	Two spikes on the shank of this worm dunker's fave hold long bait in place.	The large gap and turned-in point lock larger bait in place and hold fast.
BAITS	Live or dead baitfish and cutbait.	All live baitfish, from fathead minnows to shiners and herring.	Shiners hooked up through the lips or under the dorsal fin above the spine.	Red worms for panfish; crawlers for walleyes, trout, and catfish.	Crayfish, large shiners, and other live baitfish.
PRESENTATION	Bottom rigs work with dead bait and cutbait. Use a free line for live baitfish.	Any live-baitfish tactic, including bobbers, free lines, and bottom rigs.	Using a long pole, dip the Aberdeen hook and minnow combo in pools.	Any bait fishing tactic that involves frisky live bait.	Fish shiners under a bobber or on a free line.

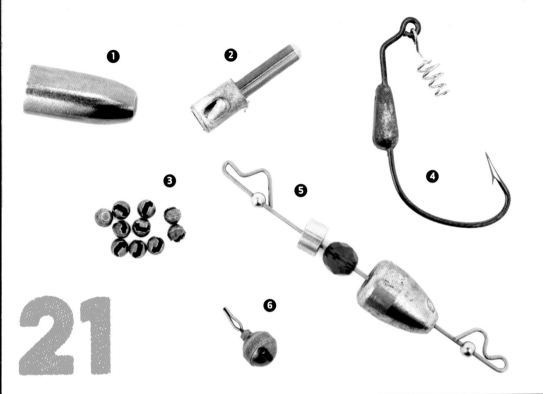

GAIN SOME WEIGHT

The weight you choose to rig a soft-plastic bait can make that lure a killer—or a dud. Compared with yesterday's sinkers, today's models are more sophisticated and specialized than ever, so it pays to invest in a variety of them. Here are six types you need in your tackle box so you can always sink to the bass's level.

1. BULLET WEIGHT Environmentally friendly tungsten bullet weights are smaller than equally heavy lead and louder when your Texas-rigged bait bumps cover.

2. INTERNAL TUBE WEIGHT Compared with a bullet weight, this sinker gives tubes a more natural appearance and a smaller profile. When you're angling for skittish bass, both advantages can pay off nicely for you.

3. SPLIT SHOT Split-shot rigs are deadly for lure-shy bass. Bullet Weights Egg Shot slides over cover more easily than round split shot, reducing snags.

4. WEIGHTED HOOK A weighted hook lets you alter a bait's action.

5. CAROLINA SINKER Noisy Carolina rigs usually work better. On Lindy's Carolina Mag Weight, magnetized steel balls separate and collide with the slightest movement to draw more bass. The weight comes preassembled.

6. DROP-SHOT WEIGHT Drop-shotting excels for finessing clear-water bass. They're denser than lead and help you "feel" what's on the bottom. The narrow, line-gripping eye eliminates the need for a knot.

22 TIE A CLINCH KNOT

This versatile terminal knot is excellent for securing your line to a hook, lure, or swivel; it's perhaps most commonly used to fasten the leader to a fly.

Pass several inches of line through the hook or lure eye (1). Next, loosely wrap the tag end around the loop you've made (2). Wind the leader several times around the loop, then pass it through the opening just below the hook (3). Pass the leader through the far end of the loop (4), and then tighten down and trim as necessary (5). The hook itself will hang from the middle of the knot.

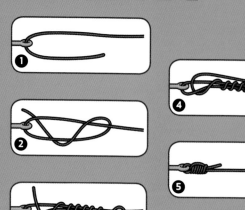

23 RIG A SLIP BOBBER

Rigging a slip bobber is a breeze. First, fasten a bobber stop on your line. Some commercial ones are on string that comes pre-knotted around a tube. Thread your line through the tube and then slide the knot off the tube and tighten. Or try what I like best: a bit of rubber tubing so small that it impedes casting very little when wound on a reel. If your slip bobber has a large hole at the top, add a small plastic bead on your line to keep the stop from sticking inside the bobber. Thread on the bobber after the bead and then tie a hook to the end of your line with two or three small split-shot sinkers spaced a few inches apart, a foot or so above the hook.

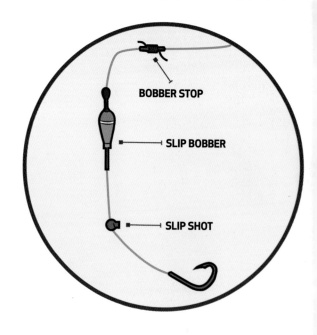

BOBBER STOP

SLIP BOBBER

SLIP SHOT

24 PROPERLY SHARPEN A FISHHOOK

Have you sharpened any lure hooks lately? Has a fish pulled a split ring open on you in the last few years? If not, it's probably because razor-edge hooks and superstrong split rings have become standard on many new lures. You do more harm than good by attempting to improve the new generation of chemically sharpened hooks, but less expensive versions normally need touch-ups. Here's how to do it right.

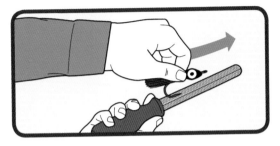

STEP 1 Hold the hook you want to sharpen by the shank between your thumb and forefinger so the bend faces inward and the point is away from you. Grasp a metal file in your other hand.

STEP 2 Brush the left side of the point away from you and down the file in one long stroke. Give it another stroke if you desire, but file any further and you'll weaken the point.

STEP 3 Repeat the first two steps for the right side and the outside of the point.

25 MAKE IT SNAPPY

Snaps that hold lures are as important as the lures themselves.

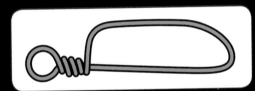

COASTLOCK SNAP Typically made of heavier gauge wire than duolock snaps, Coastlocks are staples in the saltwater world when tuna, marlin, and other big-game species are involved. Their design makes them very hard for a hard-fighting fish to pull open.

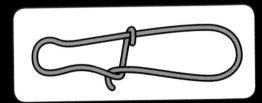

DUOLOCK SNAP Available in a wide variety of sizes, duolock snaps open wide to easily slip through the eye of any lure. Just make sure you use one strong enough for the size fish you're targeting, because they can pull open if over-stressed.

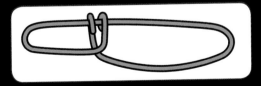

CROSS-LOK SNAP Slightly stronger than duolocks because of their design, cross-loks—even smaller models—can handle a lot of pressure. These snaps are often found on pre-made wire leaders for bluefish or muskies.

26 USE THE BEST TROUT FLY FOR THE JOB

No one fly catches all the fish all the time. Fish, ever whimsical, sometimes refuse to eat on Friday the fly they ate on Tuesday. Fishermen, ever inventive, constantly create new patterns. Tested by time, water, and fish, these are the reliable flies you need.

EGG FLY Not a fly so much as a ball of yarn, salmon egg patterns hook everything from stocked trout to native steelhead.

BLACK GHOST This classic Maine-born streamer is killer for trout holding in fast water.

GRIFFITH'S GNAT When trout are eating super-tiny bugs, it's hard to beat this classic midge pattern.

HARE'S EAR NYMPH Weighted or unweighted, these match-all bugs fool trout in any water.

DAVE'S HOPPER Most people are inclined to pick larger sizes to match big grasshoppers, but the smaller sizes may get you more strikes.

BLUE-WING OLIVE These little mayflies are ubiquitous on rivers nationwide, and they hatch almost year-round.

ZONKER A formed lead-foil underbody acts as a keel, which serves to keep this sexy streamer upright when stripped and twitched.

BEADHEAD PRINCE NYMPH Fish this generic nymph under an indicator in fast riffles and eddies. And hang on!

BLACK WOOLLY-BUGGER
This universal streamer matches everything from leeches to baitfish and often produces when all else fails.

ELK HAIR CADDIS Simply the best caddis imitation you can find. I carry light and dark styles in sizes 12 to 20.

BREADCRUST This generic wet fly caddis imitation scores big trout solo or when swung in tandem with a small streamer.

ROYAL WULFF Split parachute wings let this dry fly ride high through fast water. Use it with a dropper nymph.

COPPER JOHN This wire-bodied nymph sinks rapidly and stays deep, where many of the biggest trout lurk.

PARACHUTE ADAMS
Arguably the most versatile dry fly ever tied, the Parachute Adams' white post also makes it easy to follow on the drift.

MUDDLER MINNOW
One of the best generic baitfish imitators, this streamer shines in slow or fast water.

27 TIE A FIVE-MINUTE FLY

The Woolly Bugger is the perfect pattern for a learning fly-tier. It's big, so you can see what you're doing, and it involves only a few inexpensive materials. Most important, it's a proven producer for trout, bass, and almost anything in between. The savvy angler always has at least a few Buggers in the ol' fly box.

STEP 1 Wrap a piece of black 6/0 thread along the length of a size 10 elongated hook. Always wrap the thread away from yourself, over the top of the hook.

STEP 2 Secure one large black marabou feather at the front of the hook and wrap all the way back to the bend. Leave enough exposed to create a tail.

STEP 3 Connect a 2-inch (5 cm) piece of fine copper wire by the tail and also a strand of black chenille. Wrap the thread forward, then the chenille, but leave the wire behind. Next, tie off the chenille with a half hitch.

STEP 4 Now tie on a saddle hackle feather (black or grizzly), palmer it back (i.e., wrap with spacing), and secure this with a couple wraps of the wire. Trim the leftover hackle. Wrap the wire forward and tie it off with the thread. Trim the excess wire.

STEP 5 Finish the fly with a tapered thread head. Use a whip-finish knot, apply a dab of head cement, and you're done.

28 KNOW YOUR BUGS

Instead of grabbing a fly and hoping that you're close, get some inside information by seining a stream before you fish it. First wade out to where fish typically hold. Firmly grasp a small hand seine downstream of your feet on the creek bottom and turn over a dozen or so rocks. Bring up the net and look closely. Also check the surface flow in the current below if fish are actively feeding around you. You should pick up hatching insects, as well as any terrestrials that have the fish turned on. You don't need to be an entomologist to figure out what to do with what you seine.

 **MAYFLY NYMPHS** come in many forms depending on the particular species: crawling, swimming, and burrowing. Try to match the general size, color, and profile of the insect.

 **STONEFLY NYMPHS** are often large and can't swim, so they crawl from stream bottoms to dry land or overhanging vegetation to emerge. Match color and size to entice trout.

 **CADDISFLY NYMPHS** have two aquatic life stages. The larva lives in a tiny tube made of twigs and sand. It then seals itself into a case to pupate and grow legs and wing pads.

29 PRACTICE ANIMAL MAGNETISM

The long, flexible hair from a deer's tail is widely used in making bucktail jigs as well as streamer flies like the Clouser Deep Minnow. Deer body hair, meanwhile, is shorter, stiffer, and hollow. It can be spun around a hook shank with thread and trimmed to make floating bass bugs. In either case, you can have the satisfaction of catching fish with lures and flies made from your own trophy, if you happen to hunt. Here's a quick cut to get you there.

CUT AND CURE Start with a fresh deer tail cut at its base from the hide. Slice open the hide to expose the tailbone and remove the bone, starting at the base and working on the underside. Scrape away as much fat and tissue as possible. To get the right deer body hair, cut a few hide pieces about 4x4 inches (10x10 cm) in both white (belly) and brown (back or side) shades, and scrape. Coat the scraped hide with salt and allow to cure, which will take a few days.

COLORS TO DYE FOR After the hide dries, gently wash bucktail or body-hair patches in lukewarm water, using a standard household detergent. Rinse thoroughly to get rid of grease and grit. Air-dry the hair, unless you plan to dye it, in which case keep it wet while you ready a dye bath. Deer hair is easily colored with common fabric dyes such as Rit or Tintex. Believe it or not, one of the best dyes to use for some colors such as orange or purple is unsweetened Kool-Aid. The most useful color for both flies and jigs is natural white; save at least one tail without dyeing it. For, say, smallmouth bass jigs, you'll probably want to dye some tails in green, brown, and orange so your jigs will imitate crayfish.

A

B

C

D

E

TROPHY BUCKTAILS:
(A) Bucktail jig;
(B) Mickey fin;
(C) Frankie Shiner;
(D) Hot Lips saltwater jig;
(E) Clouser Minnow

30 JIG YOUR BUCK

Making a bucktail jig is easy. Clamp a jighead by the hook bend in a fly-tying vise or locking pliers. Fasten some fly-tying or polyester sewing thread right behind the jighead. Separate and grab a 1/8-inch-diameter (3 mm) clump of white bucktail with your thumb and index finger. Cut this clump at the base of the fibers. Hold it next to the jig—hair tips to the rear—to gauge desired hair length, then trim the butts accordingly. Now hold the clump so butts are just behind the jighead and secure butt ends of the hair fibers to the hook shank with six to eight tight turns of thread to anchor the hairs onto the hook. Continue adding clumps of hair all the way around the jig. Finish with a whip-finish knot or a few half-hitch knots. Finally, coat the thread wraps with some hard-finish nail polish.

31

CATCH A TROUT'S ATTENTION

Flies either imitate natural bugs or they attract the attention of fish. A new synthetic called Ice Dub, when wrapped into the body of a fly, does both. Classic nymph patterns like the Hare's Ear and Prince look just as realistic when they are tied with Ice Dub, yet they also flash and draw eyeballs—especially in low-light conditions—better than the same patterns tied with natural fur and feathers. In fly fishing, seeing is half of the believing equation for trout, and Ice Dub commands notice better than anything else.

32 MAKE FLIES, NOT BUGS

Winter is when many people get serious about tying flies for next spring. Make sure your materials are sealed in plastic bags together with a few moth flakes. Otherwise, dermestid beetle larvae may start chewing and destroying them. (These are the same larvae that taxidermists use to clean animal skulls.) Be especially wary if you borrow or are given a rooster neck or bucktail from someone else, or you might find your entire collection infested.

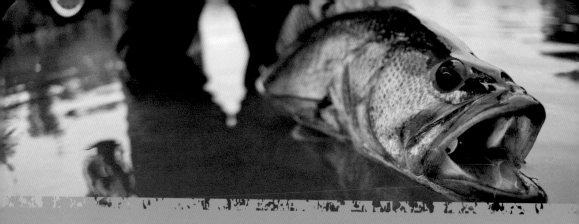

33 JOIN THE BASS BUG REVOLUTION

The essence of flyfishing for bass is a kind of laid-back antidote to trout fishing's match-the-hatch intensity. Bass bugs are fanciful rather than factual, full of wanton wiggles as they pop, slide, or slither among the lily pads of summer. Here's a close look at some of the best.

TOP PICKS Poppers and sliders are both essential patterns for topwater fishing, and new dense foam bodies float better and last longer than older cork versions. Soft silicone-rubber legs, meanwhile, add lifelike movement that drives bass nuts. Cup-face poppers make lots of surface noise when twitched, stirring up lethargic fish. Sliders, on the other hand, make a slow and quiet surface wake when stripped with intermittent pauses. Not all modern bass bugs are high

floating. The Polk's Dirty Rat swims with only its nose above water when retrieved—just like a mouse. There's also the Chubby Gummy Minnow, a fly caster's version of the soft-plastic jerkbaits used by conventional bass anglers. Its soft, shiny body is a great imitation of the threadfin shad that are common forage in many lakes.

FLY LURES Fly anglers are now imitating other bass lures, and the results can be terrific. They're heavy enough to sink but not so much that they rocket to the bottom. Because bass often hit while the fly is sinking, a slow drop can be a good thing. There are equivalents for soft-plastic worms, too, based on a long, flexible strip of wiggly rabbit fur. That soft fur has more bass-tempting wiggle in the

water than even the softest of plastics. The fly also has a lightly weighted head to give jiglike action when retrieved. Rabbit-fur flies do raise one critical point: Fur soaks up lots of water, and the weight becomes very difficult to cast with lighter gear. Although smaller, lighter bugs can easily be cast with trout tackle, bigger flies require a heavier line and rod. Eight- to 10-weight rods are not too big for larger bugs, and they're best coupled with a bass-taper fly line. This is not dainty stuff. When a 6-pound (2.75 kg) bass smashes your bug, those same heavier rods have enough power to keep the fish from diving back into cover. So not only will you have the fun of awesome surface strikes—you might even land the fish, too.

34 EXPERIENCE FATAL ATTRACTION

Absent an obvious hatch, you want a fly pattern that's buggy enough to earn interest, gaudy enough to cause a reaction strike, or just plain meaty-looking enough that the trout cannot let it float by. You want an attractor. Here are four of the best. Don't fish without them.

THE PATTERN	Rubber-Legged Stimulator	Autumn Splendor	Twenty Incher 	Mercer's Lemming
WHY IT WORKS	Replicates a range of natural insects, from stoneflies to caddis to hoppers.	A brown body gives it crayfish appeal, and the rubber legs drive trout wild.	It's a Prince Nymph on steroids with soft hackle wing accents to oscillate in water.	No natural food packs more protein power than mice; a big meal for big fish.
WHEN TO FISH IT	Spring through fall, especially midsummer.	It's not a fall-only pattern. Fish it year-round.	Year-round, but it's most deadly in spring and summer.	Summer nights when big trout are on the prowl.
HOW TO WORK IT	Dead-drift the fly tight to banks. The seductive legs will do the rest.	Bang the banks, then retrieve the fly with fast, erratic strips.	Make it the lead fly on a double rig and dead-drift it through deep runs.	Make short, erratic strips toward the shore, above runs, and around cover.
TYING TWEAK	For dirty water, increase the flash with a sparkle-dubbing body.	Remove the conehead weight for softer presentations to lake fish.	Mix and match head-dubbing colors to find the real money mix.	Dab a spot of glow-in-the-dark paint on the head so you can see it at night.

35 GET THE INSIDE SCOOP ON FLY REELS

A spinning reel that costs $30 is going to function mechanically the same as one that costs $1,000. Fly reels, however, are different. If you're in the market for a new one, understanding the advantages and disadvantages of the two most common styles of internal gears can help you determine how much to spend and which reel is best for you. It ultimately boils down to what species of fish you intend to hook, and how hard that fish is going to fight.

CLICK-PAWL DRAG In the early days of fly fishing, all reels featured a click-pawl drag. In a simple configuration, a gear fixed to the back side of the spool locks into triangle-shape clickers held in place with tension on the inside of the reel frame. When the spool turns, the clickers keep up tension to stop the line from overrunning, as well as to stop the spool from moving in reverse. Some click-pawl reels feature adjustment knobs that allow the angler to change the amount of pressure on the clickers, thus making it easier to reduce tension when stripping line off to cast, and adding it when a fish is pulling against the reel. Click-pawl drags are still popular today, but they are mostly found on inexpensive reels. Click-pawls also are typically reserved for chasing smaller fish, such as stream trout and pond bass. It doesn't make much sense to spend a ton of money on a click-pawl for small-water applications, as the reel is little more than a line holder.

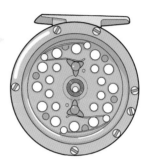

DISC DRAG Disc-drag fly reels are certainly more than line holders. These reels use a series of stacked washers sandwiched between plates covered in materials like cork or carbon fiber that be can compressed or decompressed via a drag adjustment knob to increase or decrease tension. Disc-drag systems factor in the amount of heat generated when a fish is spinning the drag quickly, as well as the torque applied during a hard run. Disc-drag reels can cost a pretty penny depending on the material used in construction. But if you're chasing salmon, steelhead, striped bass, or tuna that are going to take a lot of line off the reel, you'll want the reliability of a solid disc drag. Many disc drags are also sealed within the reel frame by a metal housing. This is particularly important to look for if the reel will be used in saltwater, as the housing keeps water out of the drag, thwarting corrosion and making sure moisture between the discs doesn't compromise the drag's performance.

36 UNDERSTAND YOUR FLY REEL

The fly reel has three basic purposes: to store line and backing, to provide a smooth drag against a running fish, and to balance rod weight and leverage. Even the most complex flyfishing reels are simpler than an average spinning reel, but it still behooves you to understand how to best utilize this vital piece of gear.

Flyfishing reels don't revolve during a cast because fly anglers strip line from the reel and let it pay out during the back-and-forth motion called "false casting." In the past, fly reels have served largely as line-storage devices with simple mechanical drags. Advancing technology and increased interest in flyfishing for big, strong-fighting fish

have led to strong drag systems that can stop fish as large as tarpon, which can reach 200-plus pounds (91 kg). Other recent developments include warp- and corrosion-resistant materials and finishes and larger arbors—the spindles around which the line is wrapped—that reduce line coils and help maintain consistent drag pressure.

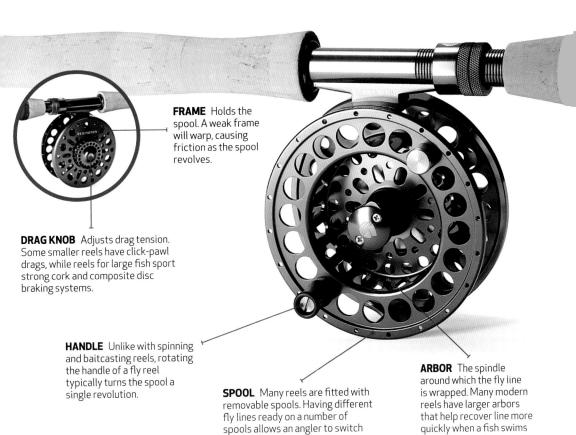

FRAME Holds the spool. A weak frame will warp, causing friction as the spool revolves.

DRAG KNOB Adjusts drag tension. Some smaller reels have click-pawl drags, while reels for large fish sport strong cork and composite disc braking systems.

HANDLE Unlike with spinning and baitcasting reels, rotating the handle of a fly reel typically turns the spool a single revolution.

SPOOL Many reels are fitted with removable spools. Having different fly lines ready on a number of spools allows an angler to switch tactics more quickly.

ARBOR The spindle around which the fly line is wrapped. Many modern reels have larger arbors that help recover line more quickly when a fish swims toward the angler.

37

GET IN LINE

Unlike a spinning or conventional outfit where the reel and bait or lure weight dictate how far you cast, when it comes to flyfishing, the reel won't gain you distance, and what's tied to the end of the line doesn't matter. What you're actually casting is the line, and the fly you choose simply makes it more or less difficult to cast that line properly. The type of water, proper presentation of certain styles of fly, and the pursuit of different species sometimes call for specialty fly lines. These are the four most common types; picking the right one will up your success with the long rod.

INTERMEDIATE LINE Often clear or light color, intermediate line is heavier than floating line but lighter than a full-sink line. This line is designed to sink slowly, allowing you to present flies to fish holding in the middle of the water column. The coloring helps it blend into the surroundings underwater, and it is widely used by saltwater flyfishermen chasing wary species like striped bass as well as freshwater anglers who strip streamers in clear lakes and deeper rivers for everything from trout to smallmouth bass to muskies. Although you can use an intermediate line to present trout flies in streams, one disadvantage is that it's harder to see the line in the water, which can make detecting subtle strikes tricky.

SINK-TIP LINE Sink-tip lines offer the ease of casting a full-floating line, with the addition of a 5- to 12-foot (1.5 to 3.5 m) tip section that sinks. These lines are popular for streamer flies that are stripped back to mimic baitfish in the water, and can also be used to fish nymphs and wet flies in deeper rivers and lakes. A sink-tip line is ideal for fishing water in the 5- to 10-foot (1.5 to 3 m) depth range, or can work in shallower water when you need to get your fly into the zone quickly. If you are floating in a drift boat and want to strip a streamer through a deep pocket, a sink-tip line will let the fly sink into the pocket fast, giving your fly maximum time in the strike zone when you have only a few seconds in which to make your presentation.

FLOATING LINE The vast majority of fly fishing situations call for a full-floating line. Whether you present dry flies on a trout stream or bass bugs on a lake, floating lines cast the easiest and most accurately. Even if they need to fish a wet fly or nymph below the surface, most fly anglers don't fish areas deeper than 6 feet or so, nor do they target fish holding higher in the water column. The 7- to 12-foot (2 to 3.5 m) leader used with a floating line is typically long enough to allow flies to reach the proper depth. Floating line also acts as its own strike indicator; when swinging a fly below the surface, keep an eye on the point where the fly line meets the water and watch for tics and stops. It's important to treat floating lines with dressing to keep them supple and slick for good castability. If they crack or lose their coating, they may not float as well. You can also find specialty floating lines that perform best in warm or cold water.

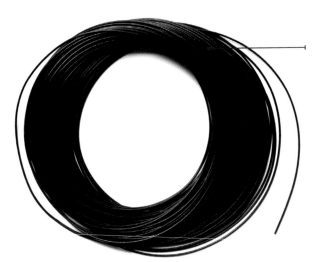

FULL-SINK LINE Although not very fun to cast, full-sink lines exist for special situations, and for the anglers who like to push the limits of fly fishing. In saltwater, a full-sink might be in order to get a fly down 20 feet (6 m) or more in a hurry to a school of bluefin tuna. In freshwater, anglers use full-sink lines to get streamers to the deepest, darkest holes in lakes and rivers where monster trout and bass live. Sinking lines are generally configured by grain, which translates to weight, thus telling how many feet or inches per second that line will sink. The drawback to a full-sink line is that it has no versatility, so while one hole in the river may call for it, you'll likely hang flies in the rocks all day in areas of shallower depths. But if you think there is a huge pike on the bottom in 25 feet (7.5 m) of water at your favorite lake and you insist on catching it on the fly, a full-sink might be the only way to get a streamer in front of its face.

38 ACCESSORIZE YOUR TACKLE BOX

You need more than lures. Here are eight items that experienced anglers always have on hand.

❶ FLASHLIGHT It's handy whenever you're out after dark, essential if you're stranded and have to signal for help.

❷ ADJUSTABLE WRENCH This has a wide variety of uses, from opening reel covers to tightening trolling-motor bolts.

❸ SPLIT-RING PLIERS They open split rings and allow you to replace hooks quickly and easily.

❹ LURE DYE With Spike-It lure dye, you can change a lure's hue in seconds.

❺ FIRST-AID SUPPLIES Don't let a minor injury ruin your day. If you bury a hook in your hand, for example, some simple supplies will let you take care of the problem on the water—and keep fishing.

❻ SPARE TREBLE HOOKS These often become dull or damaged when worked over rocks and gravel.

❼ SPARE ROD TIPS If you've never snapped off a rod tip, you will.

❽ GLUE STICK AND LIGHTER Use these to affix a new rod tip. Heat the glue stick with the lighter, apply the glue, and then slide on the new tip.

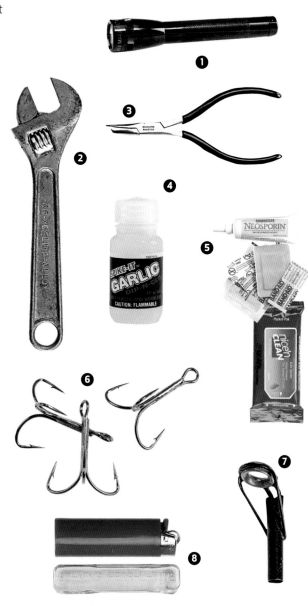

39 MAKE AN ESSENTIAL REPAIR KIT

Meet your newest fishing buddy. It's got everything you need to mend a broken rod tip, patch leaky waders, and fix broken lures. About that backlash in your baitcaster? You're on your own.

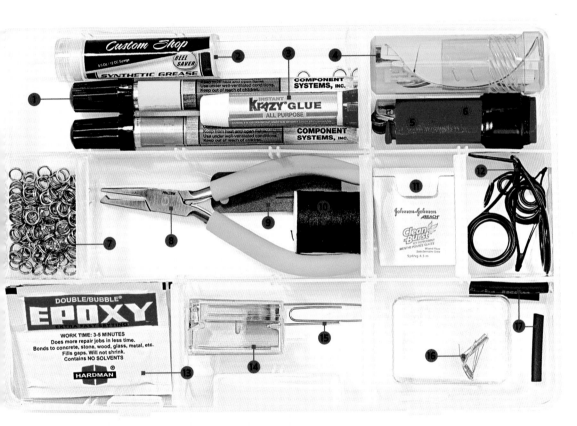

WHAT'S INSIDE:
❶ lure markers; ❷ reel oil; ❸ superglue; ❹ wader-repair kit; ❺ lighter;
❻ electrical tape; ❼ split rings; ❽ split-ring pliers; ❾ hook sharpener;
❿ rod wrap thread; ⓫ dental floss; ⓬ Fuji guide sets (spinning/baitcasting);
⓭ epoxy; ⓮ razor blades; ⓯ paper clip; ⓰ spare rod-tip guide; ⓱ shrink tubing.

40

MAKE THE ULTIMATE ICE-FISHING BUCKET

GET A BUCKET Start with a standard plastic 5-gallon bucket with a lid to haul gear and provide a seat.

ADD BUNGEE CORDS Wrapped near the rim, they secure jigging rods and tip-ups to the side of the bucket.

ORGANIZE Stash all nonmetallic items with a small tool belt fastened around the bucket. Now you've got a great place to stash things like hand warmers, tissues, plastic boxes, bobbers, and even some snacks.

VELCRO IT Attach a cushion or a piece of 3-inch (7.5 cm) foam to the lid. Using Velcro rather than glue allows you to remove the foam easily if it needs to be cleaned or replaced. And it will.

GET A GRIP The handle can also be a storage spot. Get a golf towel (one that comes with an attached clip) and snap it on. Tie on other items that you will use regularly, such as line clippers and a bottle opener.

GET ATTACHED To create handy holders for metal items, buy an assortment of inexpensive magnets. Attach them to the bucket sides with all-purpose glue, such as Gorilla Glue. Set the magnets wherever needed to keep pliers, hooks, and lures easy to reach.

41 PICK THE MOST IMPORTANT TOOL

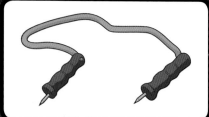

The tool that can save your life won't cost nearly as much as all your essential tackle. For a few bucks, buy a pair of ice picks. These sharp spikes are mounted to handles and tethered together on a lanyard that hangs around your neck, letting the picks dangle in easy reach on either side of your chest. Should the ice break and you fall in, get to the edge of the hole, grab the picks, reach out, and jam them hard into the stable ice. Now you have a way to pull yourself out of the hole. Even if you ice fish with friends, you should always have picks around your neck. It's a cheap way to ensure you'll be ice-fishing another day.

42

KNOW YOUR NORTHERN PIKE

Northern pike are the perfect example of a gamefish anglers either love or hate. Fishermen after bass or trout often see pike as a nuisance that steals lures and baits, decreasing the chances for the target species to get hooked. However, that voracious attitude and willingness to attack almost anything that moves have created legions of dedicated pike nuts. These fish can grow past the 40-inch (1 m) mark like their cousin the muskie, and the current world-record pike weighed 55 pounds (25 kg). Pike are also not as temperamental and hard to fool as muskies. Stocked or naturally occurring, they can be found in most reservoirs, lakes, and rivers in the northern half of the United States, with their range extending into Canada and Alaska. Find a weedbed or rocky ledge close to deep water and any live baitfish or stickbait will get crushed.

43

HIT THE ICE TWO WAYS

Whether you're after perch for the frying pan or a monster pike through the ice, there are two main attack methods that will achieve the goal. Tip-ups are metal, plastic, or wood frames that lie over a hole in the ice. On the underside, hanging in the water, is a spool loaded with line, which runs to a trigger mechanism that locks a flag on a spring or wire in a down position. When a fish grabs the bait, the trigger trips and the flag stands up. The advantage to ice fishing with tip-ups is that you can drill multiple holes and fish multiple baits simultaneously. All you have to do is sit back and watch the flags. However, tip-ups are limiting in that they only allow fishing a live or dead bait. If you want to work a jig or spoon, do so with an ice fishing rod so that you can impart action to the lure. Many seasoned ice fishermen, especially those hunting for large species, opt for rods because

they allow a change from bait to artificial presentation quickly. Rods also give the angler more control over the fish on the line, which is important if the catch is large and taking drag or putting up a hard fight. Tip-ups don't have reel, so the angler has to fight the fish by hand. That's not to say landing a trophy walleye or muskie by hand is impossible, but it definitely takes more skill.

44
PICK A ROD WITH REACH

When you're nearly on the same level as the water's surface while wade fishing, a longer spinning rod will definitely improve your game. If you need to jig a seam 30 feet (9 m) away, the added length lets you keep more line out of the water, reducing drag. Don't also increase rod stiffness, as you should be able to deliver light jigs and spinners. Opt for a 7½-foot (2.25 m) light or medium-light stick with a softer action that will send small grubs flying.

45 DRIFT ON

A few drifting tricks can radically improve your success when worm fishing, no matter what your prey. Here are two techniques endorsed by pros and weekend fishermen alike.

DRIFT AWAY

Whether you wade or fish from a boat, drifting worms is one of the great searching strategies to use when you're fishing bigger rivers. For trout, a spade-dug, 4-inch (10 cm) garden worm is the right size; for bass, walleyes, and steelhead, you'll probably find that a fat nightcrawler will be a better choice. The key is to drift the bait through feeding and holding areas, because fish in current are not going to chase down the bait like they would in still water. Use just enough weight to tick the rocks. Strikes will come as a sharp tug rather than a pull or rap. Fish the transitions, which is to say the mouths of tributaries, as well as bankside slicks and along the edges of big pools.

FOLLOW A FLOAT PLAN

Back in the day, no largemouth fisherman worthy of the name would be caught dead without a few bobbers in his tackle box. The thinking was that a bobber allowed for precise presentation, usually just above the weeds. You know what? Those guys were right ... and they still are today. Properly positioned, a nightcrawler becomes deadly bait for pond bass. The trick is to drift along a transition in weed height or density, trailing the worm behind the boat and using as little weight as possible and a quarter-size float so the fish won't feel resistance when it takes the bait. Try it at first and last light. Full sun scatters largemouths and emboldens panfish, which rip apart floating crawlers.

46 KNOW YOUR BLUE CATFISH

Head to the South and it won't be hard to find a diver who swears he's encountered a blue big enough to swallow a man in the local lake, or an angler who swears she hooked a blue so big there was no hope of winning the fight. Though man-eaters are unlikely, these fish do frequently top 100 pounds (45 kg), with the world record standing at 143 pounds (65 kg). Blue cats are natives of the Mississippi River drainage but have also been introduced to Eastern rivers and Southern lakes. To drop a jaw with a blue cat, you've got to catch one heavier than 40 pounds (18 kg), and to do that, most anglers lean on fresh-cut shad baits or live shad. Despite popular belief that catfish love stinky, rotting baits, most blue cat aces will tell you the fresher the bait, the bigger the cat. Many pros lean on heavy gear reserved for saltwater pursuits

47

KNOW YOUR RAINBOW TROUT

Originally native to the West Coast from California to Alaska, rainbow trout are now one of the most widely stocked species in the country, available in neighborhood lakes to mountain streams of the Rockies and Appalachians. Wild rainbows are particularly prized for their brute fights and aerial acrobatics on the line. Unlike brown trout, which will sometimes lie low and be choosy about meals, rainbow trout, by and large, are more aggressive. These fish will strike streamer flies and jerkbaits with crushing blows. At the same time, stocked rainbows can be fooled with a simple garden worm or be keyed into a very specific bug hatch, gently sipping flies off the surface. Of all the places these fish live, Alaska is still considered by many to be rainbow Mecca. The trout here get fat on salmon eggs, and frequently hit the 20-pound(9 kg) mark in such rivers as the Kenai.

48

TIE A TRUCKER'S HITCH KNOT

This versatile knot is great for tying down heavy or unwieldy loads for transporting. Use it to tie your canoe or kayak to a car or truck's roof racks.

STEP 1 Loosely loop your rope as shown, leaving the tail end free.
STEP 2 Feed the tail end through your anchor point and then through the loop made in Step 1.
STEP 3 Loop the free end into a half-hitch knot.
STEP 4 Tighten all knot points well for safety.

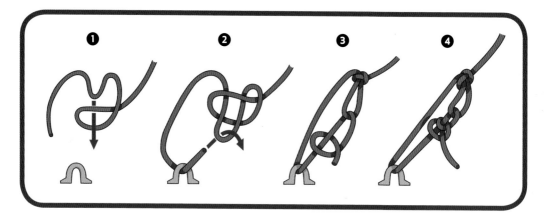

49 CAST FROM A KAYAK

For easy casting from a kayak, install a movable anchor system. Mount pulleys near both ends of the craft, run a 9/16-inch (4.75 mm) braided nylon line through them, and tie the ends to a strong metal or plastic ring. Insert your anchor line and tie it off to a deck cleat. Use the pulley line to move the ring forward or back, adjusting the anchor pull-point until the kayak is in a comfortable casting position for your target area.

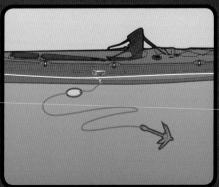

50 BACK YOUR TRAILER EASILY

Backing a boat trailer down a ramp isn't hard, but it does take practice. The key fact to keep in mind is that the trailer will always go in the opposite direction to the tow vehicle. This causes a great deal of confusion for newbies and is one of the main reasons you see guys wrestling a trailer that seems to have a mind of its own. Here's an easy way to master this maneuver:

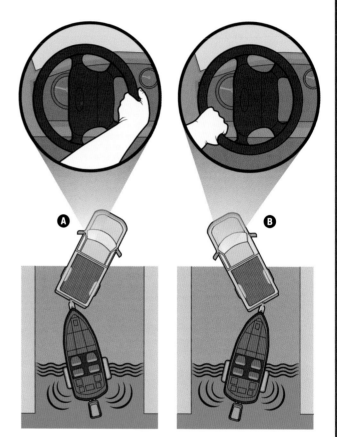

GO SOLO Before you go anywhere near the water, practice your moves in a big empty parking lot–the kind of place you'd go to teach your kid how to drive. Shift into reverse, then place your left hand on the bottom of the steering wheel. When you move your hand to the right (which turns the steering wheel and the front tires to the left), the trailer will move to the right (A). When you move your hand to the left, the wheel and front tires go right and the trailer moves left (B).

TAKE IT SLOW Most beginners back up too fast at first. Go slowly, and if the trailer starts to move in the wrong direction, stop. Pull up, straighten the trailer, and start again. Trying to correct a wayward trailer in motion will only make matters worse. Once you master the parking lot, you're ready for the ramp.

51
KNOW YOUR STEELHEAD

Steelhead are actually rainbow trout. They live in saltwater and run back into freshwater rivers to spawn. Because they dine on the ocean's nutrient-rich saltwater forage, they grow very large and fight a whole lot harder than the average freshwater rainbow. Their name comes from their chrome colorations. True salt-running steelhead are native to the Pacific Northwest, but in the 1960s, they were introduced to the Great Lakes. Though these fish don't make it to the ocean, every spring and fall they run up rivers and creeks that drain into lakes from New York to Michigan. Hooking a steelhead isn't difficult; they fall to salmon egg sacks, salmon egg flies, streamer flies swung in the current, or crankbaits. The challenge is landing one. They can rip miles of line off a reel, or run into root snarls and rock piles to shake the hook. Most steelhead hooked in rivers require the angler to chase downstream to have a chance at netting.

52
PROTECT YOUR TRAILER LIGHTS

The lights on your trailer are essential for safety. Here's how to protect them.

COOL DOWN Anglers trailering a boat to a launch ramp often forget that boat-trailer lights can burn out when the hot bulbs are submerged in water. After driving even a short distance, the trailer lights need time to simmer down. To do this properly, disconnect the trailer's electrical wiring plug from the vehicle and let the bulbs cool as you load gear into the boat before launching. Hang the wiring plug over a high point so it won't get dunked.

STAY DRY Even better, prevent electrical shorting by rigging your trailer's wiring so no junctions or terminals are ever submerged. Do this by elevating the lights on upright poles bolted to the frame. Don't join the wires in a Y-formation on the trailer body. Instead, run separate wires from each taillight all the way to the vehicle plug. For extra protection, use an outdoor extension cord rather than standard electrical wire.

TECHNIQUES

SMALL CHANGES YIELD BIG RESULTS.

In many cases, techniques are no more than subtle nuances that change the presentation of a bait or lure in a minor way. The difference in strikes between dragging a tube on the bottom and hopping it for smallmouth bass can be drastic. Learning to flip cast a jig into a tight spot instead of trying to overhand cast can result in that jig spending more time in front of the fish and less time tangled in a branch. The techniques in this chapter, broken down by species, will help you dial in your plan of attack based on elements from water depth to the time of year. The more tricks you have in your repertoire for your favorite fish, the better prepared you'll be to catch them.

53 CRANK UP YOUR SPRING

It's springtime. You've got a tackle box full of crankbaits and a whole lake in front of you. Question is, how do you make this popular lure work best during this transitional time of year? This guide will help.

SEASON AND LOCATION KEY

● **EARLY SPRING**
Water Temperature:
40°–55°F (4°–13°C)
Time of Year: February–March in the South; March–April in the North

● **SPRING**
Water Temperature:
55°–70°F (13°–21°C)
Time of Year:
March–April in the South; April–May in the North

❶ POINTS Fan your casts to the points of creek mouths and within the first quarter of creek arms; use a balsa wood–body crank. You may need spinning tackle to cast it, but it's worth it. Plastic lures may cast farther, but nothing beats the sexy wobble of a balsa wood crankbait, especially early in the season.

❷ GRAVEL AND ROCK Run a ½-ounce (15 g) lipless rattle bait over gravel and rock bottoms near the mouths of creeks. Make regular bottom contact. Sunny banks are generally more productive, as rocks trap heat.

❸ BANKS AND RIPRAP Sweep 45-degree-angle banks and riprap with a suspending crankbait, which will hover in place when you pause the retrieve. This gives sluggish bass ample time to respond. Any time you come across shallow brush, stumps, or wood, switch to a ⅜-ounce diving crank and bounce it off the structure.

❹ SUBMERGED GRASS Work over the deep edges of submerged grassbeds, which are just now beginning to grow, with a shallow-diving crankbait or lipless crank. In many lakes, grass is present down to 10 to 12 feet (3 to 3.7 m), though in especially clear lakes it could be 18 feet (5.5 m) or deeper. Tick the top of the vegetation with your lure to mimic baitfish fleeing the cover; this can trigger reluctant bass to attack.

❺ WOOD COVER Crank a tight-wiggling ¼-ounce (7 g) bait in orange and a wide-wobbling ⅓-ounce (9.25 g) in pearl red eye over wood cover. This includes stumps lining creek channels that cut through flats, brush, and windfalls and next to boat docks.

❻ GRAVEL AND CLAY BANKS Pull bass from chunk-rock, gravel, riprap, and red-clay banks with a ⅜-ounce

(10.5 g) crayfish-imitation crank that dives deeply enough through the water to bounce off the bottom.

7 GRASSBEDS Cast and retrieve a 1/2-ounce (14 g) crankbait over submerged grassbeds and along the inside edges. A crank that dives no deeper than 1 foot (30 cm) is ideal where grass grows up within inches of the surface.

8 FLOODED BUSHES When water rises above normal depth in spring, crash a heavy 3/4-ounce (21 g) lipless crankbait through submerged bushes. You'll need a stiff graphite rod and 50-pound (23 kg) superbraid line.

54 CATCH BASS WITHOUT A BOAT

Who says you need a fancy bass boat and expensive electronics to catch a hog? Learn to read your local pond, and you'll be able to hook up like a bass pro with your feet on the bank.

FIND THE CHANNEL There may be a small creek entering one end of the pond itself. Try casting a buzzbait at the mouth of the creek and in a 50-foot (15 m) circle in front of the mouth in the main pond. If that doesn't produce, work the channel edges with a weighted Texas-rigged plastic worm.

WORK ALL STRUCTURE Start looking for shoreline structure. The key is to spot something that looks different. A big rock, a solitary stump, a small point, and a stock fence extending into the water all potentially harbor bass. Work such spots first with a floating stickbait in short twitches and long pauses. Follow up with a slowly retrieved plastic worm.

SCOUT WEEDBEDS Beds of water lilies or weeds are obvious targets. The trick is to work a lure without hooking gobs of vegetation. Use a floating weedless frog, which will slide over the dense mats and can be paused and twitched in small pockets of open water.

LOOK BEFORE YOU CAST Before you walk to the bank, take a few minutes to watch the pond. You may see baitfish activity or perhaps even feeding bass. Study the shoreline for likely bass cover and decide how you'll approach it. Walk or stand in tree-shaded areas, if possible, instead of being out in the sun. This makes you less visible to fish, which also tend to lurk along shaded shorelines.

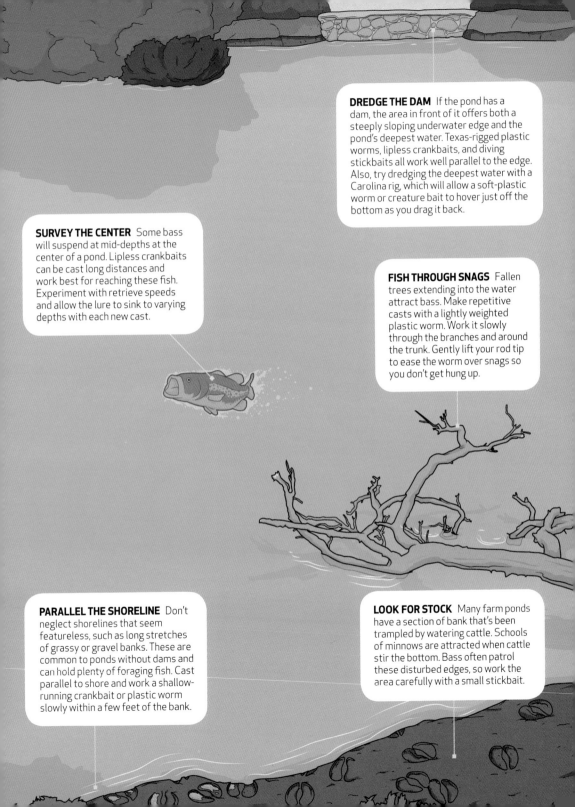

DREDGE THE DAM If the pond has a dam, the area in front of it offers both a steeply sloping underwater edge and the pond's deepest water. Texas-rigged plastic worms, lipless crankbaits, and diving stickbaits all work well parallel to the edge. Also, try dredging the deepest water with a Carolina rig, which will allow a soft-plastic worm or creature bait to hover just off the bottom as you drag it back.

SURVEY THE CENTER Some bass will suspend at mid-depths at the center of a pond. Lipless crankbaits can be cast long distances and work best for reaching these fish. Experiment with retrieve speeds and allow the lure to sink to varying depths with each new cast.

FISH THROUGH SNAGS Fallen trees extending into the water attract bass. Make repetitive casts with a lightly weighted plastic worm. Work it slowly through the branches and around the trunk. Gently lift your rod tip to ease the worm over snags so you don't get hung up.

PARALLEL THE SHORELINE Don't neglect shorelines that seem featureless, such as long stretches of grassy or gravel banks. These are common to ponds without dams and can hold plenty of foraging fish. Cast parallel to shore and work a shallow-running crankbait or plastic worm slowly within a few feet of the bank.

LOOK FOR STOCK Many farm ponds have a section of bank that's been trampled by watering cattle. Schools of minnows are attracted when cattle stir the bottom. Bass often patrol these disturbed edges, so work the area carefully with a small stickbait.

55 GET THE BASS BUGS OUT

Fly fishing for bass is a slow-paced antidote for the run-and-gun tactics of many conventional bass anglers. Sometimes it's too relaxed. Catching bass on a surface bug is so often assumed to be simple that too much is taken for granted. Pay attention to these problems here, and you'll land many more bass with surface bugs.

MIND YOUR TIP The biggest mistake most people make is holding the rod tip a few inches above the water. That leaves a short curve of slack line between it and the surface. When you strip a few inches of line to work the bug, the force of that strip is used up in shortening the slack and the fly moves only a little. If a bass does strike, that sag sometimes means you'll miss the fish. The rod tip belongs right on the water's surface when you're retrieving.

TURN IT OVER A poorly designed leader will fall back on itself as the final cast is completed, or it may flop to the left or right as the cast straightens.

In any case, your bug will land a foot or two off target. To fix this, cut 18 inches (.5 m) off the forward end of a new 8-weight bass line so the forward taper ends more abruptly. Use a nail knot to attach 3 feet (1 m) of stiff 40-pound (18 kg) test monofilament (.025-inch [.6 mm] diameter). Attach a common 7½-foot (2.25 m) knotless, tapered bass leader (.023-inch [.6 mm] butt diameter) using a blood knot, and cut a foot off the leader's 12-pound (5.5 kg) test tippet end. The combination of stiffer butt and shorter tippet does a better job than most off-the-shelf leaders in turning over a big bug at the end of a cast.

DO A LITTLE SHIMMY Countless times in clear water, I've watched the gentle splat of a landing bug bring a curious bass swimming over for a look. The bug sits still. So does the bass. After what seems like an eternity—actually about 20 or 30 seconds—I give the bug a gentle twitch, just enough to wiggle its hackle and rubber legs. Most of the time, that's enough to bring a strike.

56 DO SOME HEAVY LIFTING

Many anglers use tiny finesse baits in deep, clear bass lakes. Instead, try large, heavy baits to trigger violent strikes. Here are two favorites of the bass pros. Fish them on a medium-heavy baitcaster.

DOUBLE-HOOK SPOON Tie on a ½-ounce (14 g) slab spoon in white, gold, or silver, and drop it all the way to the bottom. Fish the spoon vertically with 1- to 2-foot (30 to 60 cm) jumps that let it pound the bottom when it touches down. It may seem aggressive, but the hits will be violent.

FOOTBALL JIG Try a ¾-ounce (21 g) peanut-butter-and-jelly football jig dressed with a 4-inch (10 cm) trailer in cinnamon–purple jelly. Cast the jig out and let it drop to bass suspended 30 to 40 feet (9 to 12 m) deep before swimming it through the area. Or bounce the jig over deep lake points.

57 KNOW YOUR LARGEMOUTH BASS

The largemouth bass is, without question, the No. 1 most sought-after gamefish species in the United States. That's because these fish adapt to and thrive in almost any climate. Whether you live in the northern reaches of Maine or the southernmost point in Texas, guaranteed there is a tiny pond, river, creek, or giant lake nearby that holds largemouths. What also makes these fish so appealing is that an angler fishing from the bank with a live minnow and a bobber has as much chance of catching a trophy as the fisherman with a new bass boat and an arsenal of the hottest new lures. Ten pounds is considered a lifetime achievement for most bass anglers, but this species grows much larger, with a 22-pound, 4-ounce (10 kg) monster caught in Japan in 2009 standing as the current world record

58 WAKE 'EM UP

We know guides who have caught 60-pound (27 kg) stripers, and a surprising number of lunker bass, by "waking" a large plug across the surface. Bass will get right in with a pack of stripers to bird-dog a baitfish school and drive it to the surface. Try using a 7½-foot (2.2 m) baitcaster and 20-pound (9 kg) mono, and cast a jointed Red Fin across a tributary point, gravel bar, or hump. With the rod tip at 10 o'clock, reel just fast enough to make the tail

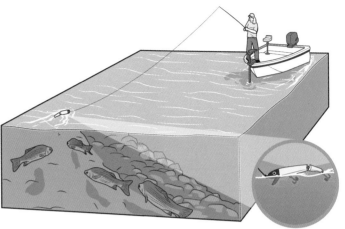

slosh back and forth, throwing a wake across the surface. Keep drag loose; your next strike could be anything from a 7-pound (3 kg) largemouth to a 40-pound (18 kg) striper.

59 STRIKE IN THE NIGHT

Big bass lose their wariness once the lights go out, and if your lake is under pressure during the day, topwater action can be stellar after dark. The two most productive nighttime bass lures are black buzzbaits and jitterbugs, but since you won't see the strike, you can't just swing away when you hear the hit. Here's how it's done.

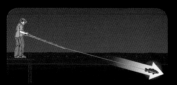

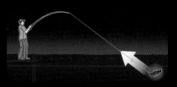

RESIST THE SET It's dark, so when you hear the strike, you won't know if the fish just knocked the lure or pulled it under. Despite what your instincts tell you, don't set. Do nothing for a moment

BE SURE Reel just enough line to pick up any slack. Then wait for the rod to load. If the fish drops the lure and you rear back, you'll have hooks flying at your face. Make sure you feel the fish first

TAKE IT SLOW Sweep the rod up slowly. The bass has had time to "walk away" with the lure and to apply pressure against the line, so there's no need to swing the rod with all your might

Pitching is an underhand baitcasting skill that's perfect for delivering bass jigs or weighted creature baits in heavy cover. It's effective from about 10 to 50 feet (3 to 15 m). You can make a pitch while standing on a boat deck, and you can practice indoors with a hookless casting weight because extremes of force and distance aren't required.

THE SETUP Heavy-cover fishing requires strong line—20- to 25-pound (9 to 11 kg) test mono (1). Start with a ¾- to 1-ounce (21 to 28 g) lure in your non-casting hand, about even with the reel. While keeping slight tension on the line with your off-hand, put the reel in free-spool and press your casting thumb against the spool to prevent any movement.

THE SWING Hold the rod at waist level, extended straight out in front of you (2). Your casting-arm elbow should be bent and relaxed. Let go of the lure to start a pendulum-like swing. As the lure swings, raise the rod upward and outward by about a foot. Release thumb pressure on the spool so the lure flies with a low trajectory. If it lands right in front of you, you released the spool too soon. A high-flying lure means you let go too late.

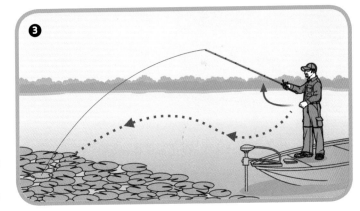

THE LANDING As the lure reaches the target you're aiming for, you'll want to thumb the spool to slow its flight and lower the rod slightly so the bait hits the water with a gentle blip (3). Remember that you're swinging the lure to make this cast, not throwing it.

61 THAW OUT A TROUT

In early spring, when ice is melting, ponds and small lakes are great places to fish. And, with oxygen confined to the surface layer, most prey are in depths of less than 10 feet (3 m). Trout are rarely far away. The most effective tactic may be to fish from the bank when so many trout are within easy casting range. Start early, because the period during and just after ice-out can be absolutely hot. It's essential that you cast in the right places. This illustration shows you where.

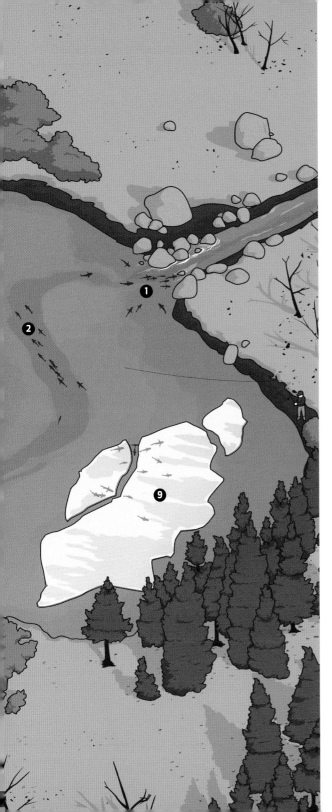

1. CREEKS Rainbows, cutthroats, and baitfish stage off creek mouths prior to spring spawning. Hit these spots with streamers, spinners, salmon eggs, or egg flies. Fish may also move into creek outlets if they find spawning habitat, so try the first quarter mile of the creek, too.

2. CREEK CHANNELS In stream-fed, man-made still waters, look for creek channels cutting through shallow flats. The deeper water offers trout a natural ambush point. Hang bait in the middle or ply the edges with streamers, Woolly Buggers, or spinners.

3. WEEDBEDS Aquatic vegetation dies back in winter, depriving insects of cover and exposing them to trout. Work dragonfly nymph patterns just above the dead weeds, or bottom-fish with waxworms and hellgrammites. You can find the beefy grubs for bait underneath woody debris.

4. DEADFALLS AND TIMBER Downed wood is a magnet for insects, trout, and bait (such as minnows and nightcrawlers). Fish it with shallow-running stickbaits or a Woolly Bugger on the fly rod.

5. SHALLOW BAYS The first areas to warm up in the early spring, skinny-water bays can be prospected with leech streamers or weighted nymphs. Stay on the lookout for cruising trout and intercept them by casting well ahead of their line of travel.

6. MUDFLATS Bloodworms and bright-red midge larvae inhabit the soft, silty bottoms on the flats. Rig a small San Juan Worm under an indicator or a live redworm under a bobber, riding it just off the bottom. Cast and let it drift with the wind.

7. NEW GROWTH From shore, cast out into open water past the new growth of reeds or rushes. Use a strip-and-pause retrieve with a damsel nymph, gold-ribbed Hare's Ear, Prince nymph, or leech streamer on the fly rod.

8. BARS AND MIDWATER SHOALS Work these areas by casting to the shallow water and retrieving into the deep water. Try a fly pattern like a midge larva or pupa, allowing it to sink to the bottom on a 12- to 14-foot (3.6 to 4 m) leader and working it back glacially slow.

9. ICE SHEETS As the thaw begins, look for open water between ice sheets and the shoreline, particularly in shallows adjacent to deep water. Some anglers cast baitfish imitations onto the ice shelf, then drag them into the water and begin their retrieve.

62 SPOT AND STALK TROUT

The secret to catching big wild trout often comes down to identifying a single target and then dissecting the fish's feeding rhythm. There is no immediate gratification here. This kind of fishing requires patience and stealth—but the prize is worth the wait.

drifting insects? Does the fish prefer prey off to one side or directly in front of its snout? Does it slurp up a mouthful of spinners or sip in singles? Pay attention to these feeding patterns and factor them into your presentation.

CALCULATE THE ANGLES
Put the fly 2 feet (60 cm) in front of the fish. A tighter cast will spook it. A longer cast could require too much mending to stay drag free. If you mess up, don't fire out a cast to cover up. Give the fish time to settle.

STALK INTO POSITION
On broken pocket water, the rippled surface allows a closer approach (A). Cast from straight downstream to keep your line out of mixed currents, but beware of small "lookout" trout (B) that will spook into the head of the pool. If you're fishing slick pools or spring creeks, don't push too close. Anglers casting wet flies should post across and slightly upstream (C) of the fish for drifts that keep the leader, tippet, and any split shot outside the trout's view.

MATCH THE RHYTHM
Does your trout rise to every morsel of food, or every few seconds, or every few

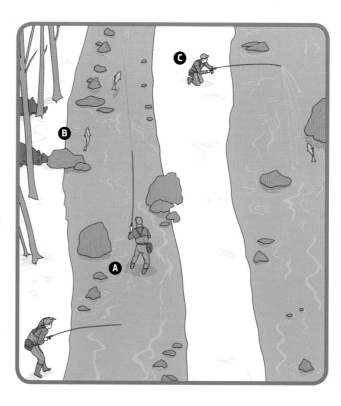

63 PERFECT THE PARACHUTE CAST

The biggest trout hold in deep water, a situation that calls for heavily weighted flies, but you need to get deep with as little weight as possible. To do this, use the parachute cast, which produces enough slack to let the fly sink unhindered by drag. Only a small amount of lead will be needed.

STEP 1 Make a standard overhead cast, aiming for a point about 10 feet (3 m) above the water.

STEP 2 Stop your forward stroke around the 12 o'clock position.

STEP 3 As the line passes overhead, snap the rod forward to the 10 o'clock position.

STEP 4 Instead of straightening out, the fly line will hinge toward the water, dropping the fly and leader vertically onto the surface.

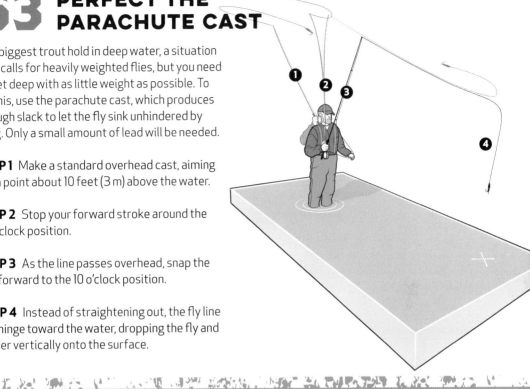

64 MASTER THE MEND

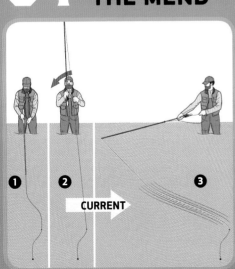

CURRENT

The key to the perfect drift is mending the line—keeping the fly line upstream of the dry fly (or strike indicator when you are nymph fishing). If the fly line gets downstream, it will grab the current and cause the fly to drag.

An ideal "mend" involves lifting the fly line from downstream and placing it upstream, without moving the fly or indicator. The most common mistake is getting jerky and trying to whip the line with the rod from chest level.

Fly rods are long for a reason. When you start the mend, lift the rod tip just high enough to pick the fly line off the water, but not so high you disturb the leader (1). With your rod tip straight up, swing it across your face from downstream to upstream (2). Gently lay down your line to the upstream side of your fly or indicator (3). In faster water, "kick" that rod over with more force.

65 FLY IN THE COLD

Trout feeding patterns change when temperatures drop and insect life cycles slow down, so you'll have to alter your tactics a bit. One of these three approaches should coax a few fish from their icy lies.

SMALL AND SLIM (A) On most winter trout streams, tiny mosquito-like midges are the most active and available food form. Standard midge pupa patterns—such as Brassies and Serendipities—can be effective. So can slim-bodied nymphs, such as the Flashback Pheasant Tail. But size is often more important than the specific fly. Think small, and go for patterns in sizes 18 to 22 on 5X to 7X tippets.

HIGH AND DRY (B) Low, clear winter water can make those occasional rising fish ultra-cautious. A size 18 or 20 Parachute Adams or Parachute Black Gnat, or a Griffith's Gnat in sizes 18 to 22, will cover a hatch of midges or, on some rivers, blue-wing olive mayflies. Keep a low profile and use long, fine leaders.

BIG AND GAUDY (C) If the microflies aren't bringing them in, you might want to try the other extreme and go large—leeches and streamers up to size 4 or so. I hooked my largest winter trout on an ordinary No. 8 black Woolly Bugger. Fish near the bottom and dead-drift with occasional short twitches.

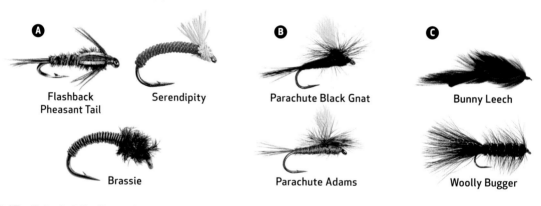

A Flashback Pheasant Tail

Serendipity

Brassie

B Parachute Black Gnat

Parachute Adams

C Bunny Leech

Woolly Bugger

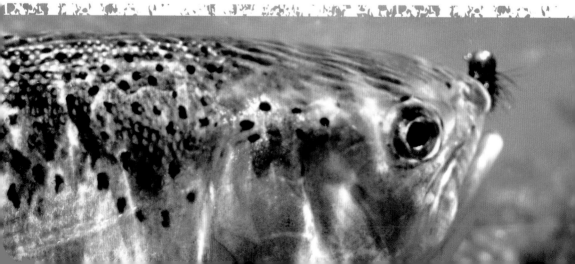

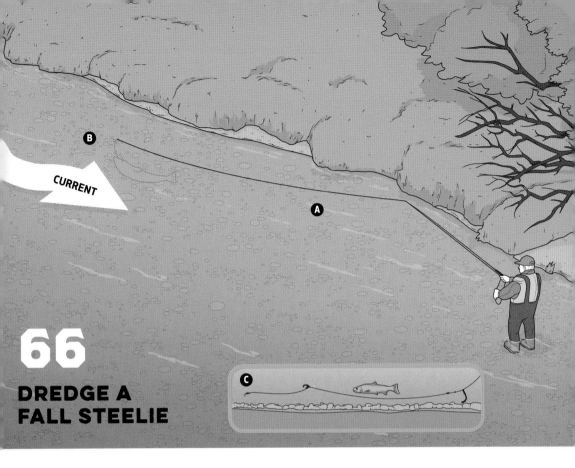

CURRENT

B

A

C

66

DREDGE A FALL STEELIE

Fall steelhead anglers typically cover water with cross-stream casts until a fish hits. Instead, try putting the fly right in front of the fish from directly downstream.

GETTING DOWN Pattern choice matters, but presentation is the real key. Put the nymph 4 to 8 inches (10 to 20 cm) above bottom, which means adding weight to your line. An unweighted fly moves more naturally than a weighted one, so try a slinky weight attached to the leader butt. The setup lets you easily change the weight as river conditions dictate.

DEAD-DRIFTING When water temperatures dip below 50 degrees (10°C), dead-drift a nymph on a 9½-foot (3 m) (or longer) 7- or 8-weight rod with a small-diameter shooting line (A) rather than a

traditional weight-forward floating fly line. The small line allows for quieter entry of the flies on the cast (no line slap to spook fish) and offers less resistance in the water, which makes it easier to get a drag-free drift. Don't false cast. Simply pick up the line and shoot it directly upstream (B). Casting with the added weight is smooth and effortless. This is a great way to work a tree-choked stream that routinely snags back casts. As a go-to rig, pros recommend an 8- to 10-foot (2.5 to 3 m) butt section that ends with a bead and barrel swivel (C). A slinky weight slides freely on the butt section via a snap. To the swivel, tie on a 3- to 6-foot (1 to 2 m) leader; onto this, knot a chartreuse caddis nymph. Run 17 to 24 inches (43 to 60 cm) of line from the eye of this fly, then attach a stone-fly nymph. The long, light tippet offers little water resistance and sinks quickly.

67 FOLLOW THE CRAPPIE HIGHWAYS

As crappies follow creek channels to spawning water, they stop at staging or rest areas. Isolated wood cover, underwater stumps along bends, and points are all good spots to find fish. The warmer the water temperature, the closer they'll be to spawning areas.

Reservoir crappies typically winter on deep main-lake structures like river-channel dropoffs, submerged roadbeds, and offshore humps. They're often 25 to 50 feet (7.5 to 15 m) deep. As the lake gradually warms in early spring, crappies gravitate toward shallower water, following predictable migration routes that lead to their eventual spawning areas.

This migration takes place in waves rather than all at once. Initial activity occurs when lake waters reach 55 to 58 degrees (12° to 14°C). By the time the lake hits 65 degrees (18°C), expect to experience some truly awesome crappie fishing if you target this pattern.

68 SLIDE A GRUB

Here is a pattern for prespawn slab crappies. Begin at a point leading into a major tributary arm, using your graph to locate a channel or ledge with a sharp dropoff (say, 8 to 18 feet [2 to 5.5 m]). Use marker buoys to delineate the structure and key pieces of submerged cover that you spot on the screen. Then back off the boat and cast a grub to the top of the dropoff, letting it fall down the slope on a tight line. If most of the strikes occur on top of the ledge, swim the grub just off the bottom with a slow, steady retrieve. You might not feel a bite because crappies may pick up the grub and swim toward you. If you see the line jump or lose contact with the lure, set the hook.

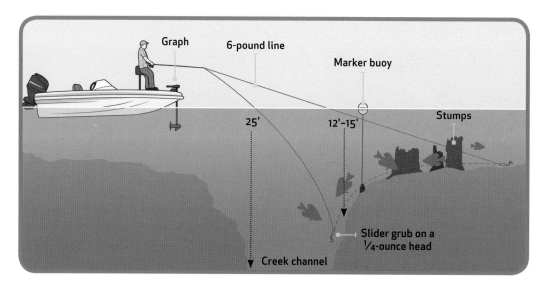

Graph 6-pound line Marker buoy

25' 12'–15' Stumps

Slider grub on a
¼-ounce head

Creek channel

GET INTO THE GRASS

When crappies are spawning, concentrate on narrow bands of grass near the shoreline. The fish hold along the inside and outside edges of the greenery, with bigger fish favoring the deeper outside edge of the grass.

Your best strategy here begins with lure selection. The key is to cast a $1/16$-ounce (1.75 g) jig dressed with a curly-tailed grub over the grass to the bank. Slowly reel the grub to the inside edge and let it sink to the bottom. If that doesn't get a strike, try pulling the jig over the vegetation and letting it sink on outside edge.

To dupe postspawners, by contrast, use a $1/16$- or $1/32$-ounce (1.75 or 1 g) tube. You can fish these baits on 6-pound line and an 11-foot (3.4 m) crappie rod with a spinning reel. Easing within a rod's length of trees standing in water 4 to 12 feet (1.25 to 3.5 m) deep, or holes in milfoil beds, slowly lower the jig straight down into the water, about 6 to 10 inches (15 to 25 cm). A crappie will often rise up and hit it. If that doesn't coax a bite, you may have luck by dropping the jig down 1 foot (30 cm) and holding it there for another 30 seconds. Repeat this process until the jig touches bottom. Then crank the jig up and fish another tree or hole in a grassbed.

70 CATCH YOUR BIGGEST BLUEGILL OF THE YEAR

Anyone can catch bluegills when they're on the bed. But you can land some of the biggest fish of your life long before the nesting season—and before the lake gets slammed with competing anglers—when the water is still chilly. Find the fish, dangle a tasty morsel inches from their noses, and wait for a bite. It's like ice fishing on open water.

To catch these fish, you need a long cane pole or a jigging pole, some jigs, and waxworms. That, and some free time. A $\frac{1}{16}$- to $\frac{1}{32}$-ounce (1.75 to 1 g) jig tipped with a waxworm is the proven standard. A plain painted ballhead jig will do, but dressed jigs with marabou, tinsel, or duck-feather skirts slow the fall rate and provide added attraction.

For fishing cover visible from the surface, a collapsible 12-foot (3.6 m) jigging pole works

very well. A seasoned cane pole also does the job. No reel is required, especially when you're fishing shallower than 10 feet (3 m). When you find the right depth, just tie that amount of line to your pole, and you're all set. You'll snag a lot of jigs in the thick stuff, so 6-pound (2.7 kg) braided line is handy for straightening hooks and saving jigs.

To probe submerged cover right under the boat in open water, make a near 180 in your tackle choice. Rather than a long crappie pole, a short, supersensitive spinning rod with an ultralight reel is best; my favorite rod length is 5 or 6 feet (1.5 to 1.8 m). I've even used ice-fishing tackle to fish rock piles. Small-diameter braid is still OK, but finicky fish, clear water, and small spinning reels prone to tangling line may require a switch to monofilament.

71 DROP IN ON SPRING 'GILLS

THE AREA When water temps reach the low to mid 50s (10°C) in spring, bluegills move out of their deep-water haunts and cling to cover in mid-depth waters (7 to 10 feet [2 to 3 m]) near favored spawning grounds. Head back to your favorite summertime bluegill beds, find the closest area of deep water, and search for nearby cover in those depths. That's likely where the bluegills will be. Experimenting with different depths is the key.

THE COVER Bluegills live their entire lives in fear of being eaten by something else, so think cover when fishing for them anytime outside the spawn. This could be weeds, brushpiles, dormant lily pads, submerged rock piles, a boat dock, or pier pilings. So long as it provides adequate cover at the right depth, bluegills will gravitate toward it.

THE APPROACH The combination of heavy cover, deep water, and sluggish fish that feed by sight is a situation that begs for vertical jigging. To fish cover that's visible from the surface of the water, stay several feet away from your target and make a slow, controlled drop with the cane pole. Alternately, you can get right on top of submerged cover in open water and fish it vertically with the short spinning rod.

THE TECHNIQUE Ease the jig into the water and slowly lower it, keeping the line taut. Bluegills may hold at any depth alongside the cover, and they often hit as the jig is falling. When you get a bite, note how deep you've lowered your jig; the next bite will likely be around the same depth. Tighten the line to set the hook at even the slightest peck.

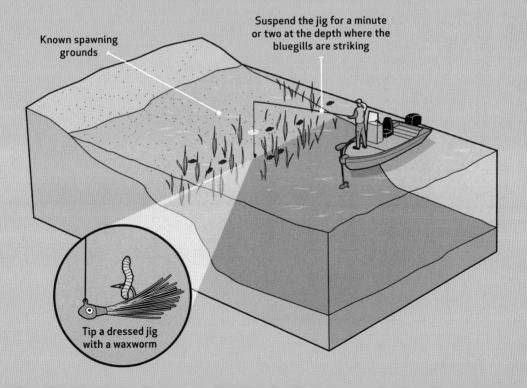

Known spawning grounds

Suspend the jig for a minute or two at the depth where the bluegills are striking

Tip a dressed jig with a waxworm

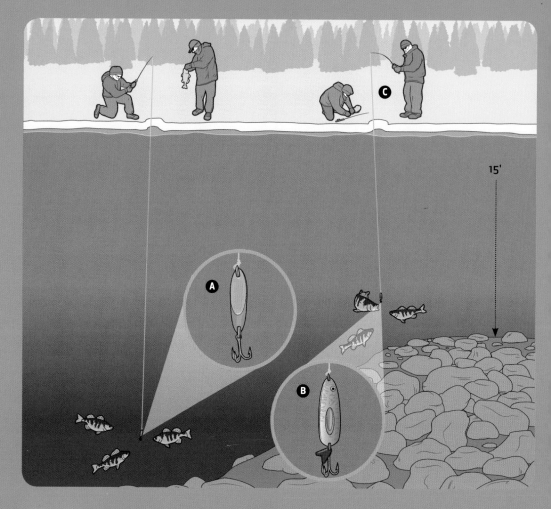

72 TAG-TEAM WINTER PERCH

Jumbo winter perch travel in pods numbering from a couple of fish to a dozen or so and tend to enter and exit the scene in a burst. Try this "firefighting" technique with a partner—as one of you unhooks, the other instantly fires back down the hole to pick off another fish.

GO DEEP Deeper than 15 feet (4.5 m), you really need a lure that will get down fast (A). Opt for a heavier metal jig that's slim and hydrodynamic. If you want to tip it with bait, waxworms are a good choice since they don't resist water like a minnow.

WORK THE SHALLOWS In water less than 15 feet (4.5 m) deep, use an aggressive flash spoon and something that gets up and down in a hurry but also sparkles enough to hold fish and draw other transient pods (B).

MOVE QUICKLY Tag-teaming perch works best on big fish that advance with zeal but are sure to vanish, and it's effective both shallow and deep. The key is to get the second bait down as soon as the first fisherman reels up (C). Try this during peak feeding hours, like dusk and midmorning.

73 TAKE A SHOT IN THE DOCK

This slingshot technique sends a light jig into tight spaces—under a dock, overhanging limbs, or blowdowns. Use a 5-foot (1.5 m) spinning rod and a closed-face spinning reel, preferably with a front trigger.

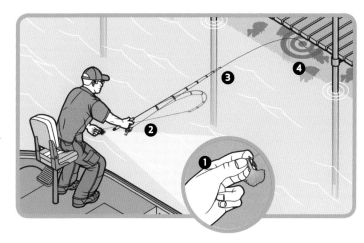

STEP 1 Let out enough line so the jig hangs parallel with the bottom rod guide. Hold the jighead in your left hand between your thumb and index and middle fingers, with the hook pointing out to avoid getting snagged on the release. In your rod hand, keep your right index finger on the trigger, which unlocks the spool.

STEP 2 Lower the jig to your left side and extend your right arm out, keeping the rod angled toward the water. As your arm extends, it will create a bend in the rod. Do not create tension by pulling on the jig. Continue to bend the rod by extending your arm until the face of the tip-top guide is parallel to the water's surface.

STEP 3 Once the rod is fully drawn, your arms should not change position. When you're ready to aim, point the rod tip at your target spot by turning your entire upper body.

STEP 4 Release the jig and the reel trigger at the same time to shoot. If the jig goes high, you probably broke your left wrist when you let the jig go. If the jig whizzes back at your head, you fired the trigger too late. The jig should fly straight and low to the water.

74 GET POST-ICE AIR

There is often a burst of good fishing on Northern lakes about three weeks after ice-out, when surface water reaches 39 degrees (4°C). At this temperature, water reaches its greatest density and sinks to the bottom, oxygenating the lake at all levels; fish throughout the lake are activated by the extra oxygen.

75 GO LONG, WIDE, AND DEEP FOR WALLEYES

In late spring to early summer, the big postspawn female walleyes are suspended in open water. To find these fish, cover as large a swath of water as you can—up to 200 feet (61 m) wide, from top to bottom. Set the shallowest baits far to the sides of your boat to avoid spooking fish feeding near the surface.

STEP 1 This setup requires four side-planer boards. Install three adjustable rod holders along each gunwale. The two flat-line rods lie parallel to the water at 90 degrees. The next two holders angle rods at 65 degrees. Those nearest the bow keep the rods up at 45 degrees.

STEP 2 Fish 10-pound (4.5 kg) monofilament on all six trolling rods except for one of two flat-line rods. Spool this one with 10-pound

(4.5 kg) braided line, which has less resistance in the water and will get the crankbait on this rod running deeper than any of the others.

STEP 3 Fish the same lure on every rod. Long, slender crankbaits with large diving bills work well. In stained water, try hot pink or orange. On sunny days, use metallics, and in clear water, try white or pearl.

STEP 4 Trolling at 1.5 to 1.7 mph (2.4 to 2.7 km/h), set the rods closest to the bow first and work down to the stern. Reels with line counters will help achieve the desired distance when sending the lures back. The longer the line, the deeper the baits will run. If one depth seems to be producing results consistently, reset the other lines to match that depth.

76 FISH A WEED-CUTTER RIG

Casting spinner rigs allows you to fish for walleye in areas you can't target when trolling. On a straight retrieve, the spinner's oscillating blade clears a path for the hook and bait. Here's how:

THE TACKLE Start with a 6- to 7-foot (1.8 to 2 m) medium to medium-heavy spinning rod (A) with fairly stiff 10-pound (4.5 kg) mono superline.

THE RIG Use a snell knot to tie a No. 2 to No. 4 wide-gap hook to a 12- to 24-inch (30 to 60 cm) leader of 10- to 14-pound (4.5 to 6.3 kg) test fluorocarbon (B). The shorter leash (trolling spinner rigs are 30 to 40 inches [76 to 100 cm]) casts smoothly, is easy to control in shallow and rough water, and permits quick hooksets. String six beads above the hook and add a No. 5

Colorado blade. Tie free end to a barrel swivel. Slip a ⅛- to ¼-ounce (3.5 to 7 g) pegged bullet sinker onto the main line before attaching it to the open end of the barrel swivel.

THE BAIT If you're using a minnow, run the hook down its throat and out the back of its head. Penetrate a leech just past the sucker or go with half a nightcrawler, hooked deeply through its thicker-skinned head (C).

THE TARGET Cover a weedbed by casting into thin spots, particularly those along and just into the outer edge, and into clearings. Bring it back straight and methodically, to halfway through the water column. A spinner blaring through the weeds elicits a quick reaction. Fish hit on instinct.

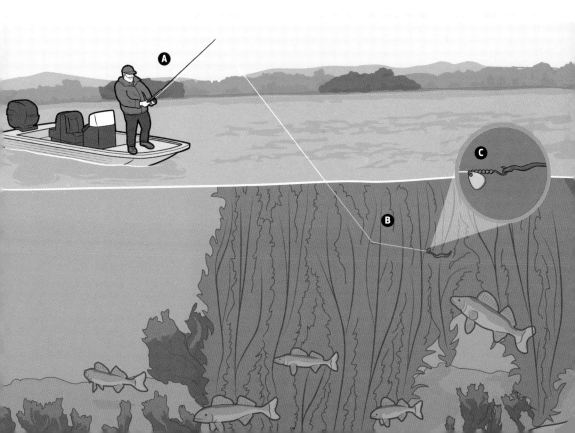

77 WEED OUT TROPHY WALLEYES

Many anglers consider June to be an unparalleled time for walleye fishing. The shallows teem with forage, and water temperatures range from the 60s to mid 70s (15° to 21°C), which is optimum to livable for a walleye. Weeds come up, lending protective cover and shade, and the walleyes take notice—and residence.

Certain weeds are better than others. True broadleaf cabbage establishes in 6 to 12 feet (2 to 4 m) of water over sand, gravel, and marl. Walleyes prefer forest-like stands, but if those are not an option, a fistful of plants in a pasture of single weeds can draw them in like a magnet. Coontail is another gem, with its lattice of Christmas-green whorls. In its most dynamic form, coontail grows in dense mats in 5 to 9 feet (1.5 to 3 m) of water.

Nothing outshines the jig-and-minnow rig here. It perfectly mimics what the fish are after, and you can fish it many different ways by varying your stroke and speed. My preference is a long-shank jig with a shiner. Thread the minnow on the hook to foil short nips. Use the electric trolling motor to crawl along and pitch the jig to weed edges or into a field of short vegetation. Swim and hop it back, bumping weed stalks and the bottom. Keep your line taut and the bait in constant motion. Weed-dwelling walleyes are aggressive fish; they'll catch up.

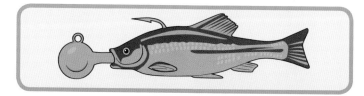

78 KNOW YOUR WALLEYE

The largest members of the perch family, walleyes can be found throughout much of the United States in small ponds and rivers to neighborhood lakes. Big fish, however, are found in more abundance in large, deep bodies of water such as reservoirs, lakes with serious acreage, or major river systems. Walleyes have exceptional night vision and frequently hunt after dark, making nighttime trolling with crankbaits highly effective. If trolling isn't your game, you can cast twitchbaits or bounce the bottom with leeches. Walleyes are also a primary target of ice fishermen because they readily strike even when the water is at its coldest. These fish have keen hearing as well as eyesight, which can make them extra-sensitive to engine noise. Pro tip: You're mostly likely to catch the biggest fish in a given area first, as the

79 DO A FALL MINNOW DOUBLE-TAKE

In the fall, walleyes come out of their summer funk and feed ravenously before ice-up. Here's how to make the most of the occurrence, whether you're fishing lakes or rivers.

LAKE FISHING Look for walleyes in lakes and reservoirs during mid-fall in water 25 to 45 feet (7.5 to 14 m) deep where dropoffs of 60 feet (18 m) or more are close by. Until ice-up, you'll get good results with a basic Lindy rig—a walking sinker and a leader with a hook—with a live 4- to 7-inch (10 to 18 cm) chub. The Lindy rig lets you drag a bait along bottom; the sliding sinker helps you feel delicate takes. You'll need a 1-ounce (28 g) weight to maintain bottom contact at these depths if there's any wind at all. Using a bow-mounted electric motor, slowly drag the walking sinker in a zigzag course along the lip of dropoffs where you've marked walleyes. Once you feel a bite, let it run for 20 seconds, reel up the slack, and make a sweeping hookset.

RIVER FISHING Walleyes gang up in the tailwaters of dams and in deep river bends when water chills in autumn. Pros rely on 1/8- to 3/8-ounce (3.5 to 11 g) standup jigs to catch these fish. The design puts the hook in an upright position to reduce snags. The teeter-totter action imparts more movement to the bait. Use the lightest jig that maintains bottom contact and tip the hook with a 5- to 6-inch (13 to 15 cm) sucker minnow. Work the jig with a slow lift-drop action. Fish the jig vertically 10 to 30 feet (3 to 9 m) deep on spinning tackle and 10-pound (4.5 kg) monofilament. Drift backward with the current, and use a bow-mounted electric motor to slow the boat and keep the line vertical. When you feel a hit, lift the rod straight into the air to set.

80 LAND A PIKE OR MUSKIE FROM YOUR KAYAK

The stakes are higher when you're fishing from a kayak—after all, you can't get much closer to your fish! Here's how to land a toothy monster without falling overboard.

GETTING IN POSITION Let the fish get tired enough to handle—but not so worn out as to prevent a healthy release. Straddling the kayak will give you leverage and better balance. Make sure that all landing tools are within reach but out of the way. Because you're so low to the water, a net is rarely necessary. With the fish beside the boat, turn on the reel's clicker. Keep at least a rod's length of line out; too much line tension loads up the rod and could result in getting yourself impaled by a hook.

LANDING YOUR FISH It's usually when you lift a pike or muskie that they thrash about. Keep your eye on the lure. Holding the rod in one hand, grab the back of the fish head, just behind gill plates. Pin especially big fish against the kayak. Once fish is stabilized, pop reel out of gear and set rod in a rod holder. Use a fish gripper to lip fish. Slide a hand below the belly to support the fish as you lift it out of the water.

81 PACK THE PLIERS

Pike will bite through just about anything they're offered, so watch your fingers when handling them. If the pike is under 10 pounds (4.5 kg), you can grip it across the back of the head, behind the eye, or over the back of the gill plate. Bigger pike should be netted and subdued with a firm grip while in the net. Needle-nose pliers are a must; jaw spreads can also come in handy. Pinch down the barbs of your lures to expedite extractions.

82 HOOK A HARD-TO-CATCH TROPHY PIKE

Early autumn can be prime season for chasing trophy northern pike. Cooler water temperatures have these fish actively working the shallows, fattening themselves up for the approaching freeze. They are also notoriously sensitive and spooky, so long casts and realistic bait presentations are critical. Here's how to catch them.

THE TACKLE Plan to use a relatively long swimbait rod—think 7-foot, 11-inch or 8-foot (2.4 m) — with a medium to fast action and a fairly flexible tip section (A). The longer rod allows you to wake baits from a distance by holding the tip high and helps you add distance to your cast. Match that with a reliable low-profile baitcasting reel.

THE RIG Large pike can get line-shy. You need a wire leader (B), but try to minimize the gaudiness of the transition from line to leader. Use 12- to 15-pound (5.4 to 6.8 kg) mono, and attach the leader with an albright

knot instead of a swivel so as to reduce unnecessary hardware in the water.

THE BAIT Use a bait that sinks slowly to work different depths (C). Swimbaits can be particularly deadly in the fall. Don't be afraid to go large, 7 inches (18 cm) or longer. Match colors to the predominant forage for pike.

THE TARGET Fall pike are in ambush mode and not typically cruising, so key on edges with relatively long casts: points near shallow bays, weedlines, and dropoffs (D). Let your bait sink well into the water column (about 3 feet or 1 m), then use slow, twitchy retrieves. Also look for transitions where clean water meets dirty water, and probe the clean edges.

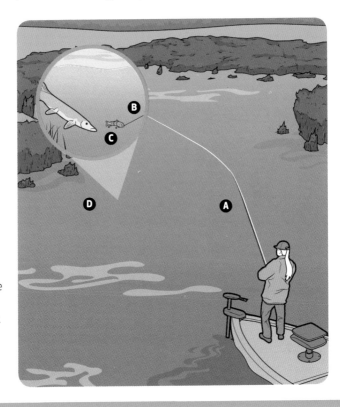

83 LURE A BIG BAD PIKE

White, yellow, and chartreuse are ideal pike lure colors, probably because they resemble the belly of a struggling food fish. Try these on for size:

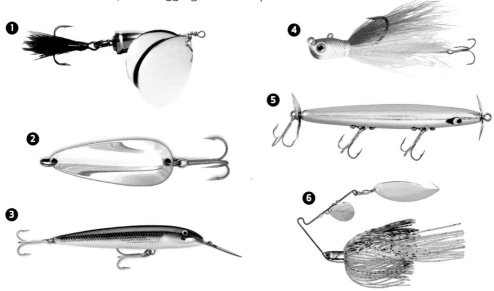

1. IN-LINE SPINNER In early spring, before weed growth becomes a factor, focus on covering water. Bigger spinners are a top choice here because the weight lets you cast them farther and the blades throw more flash. Retrieve the spinner steadily, just fast enough to keep it off the bottom.

2. SPOON Start by steadily and slowly reeling, just fast enough to keep the spoon wobbling. If that doesn't produce, try a "flutter retrieve," using a jigging motion as you reel.

3. LARGE PLUG Begin with a steady retrieve. If that doesn't work, try stop-and-start reeling. Early in the season, use a shallow runner. As waters warm up, go to a crankbait or a soft-plastic swimbait that runs in the 10-foot (3 m) range.

4. JIG As the temperature in the shallows reaches 60 degrees (15°C), pike begin to set up shop along 6- to 10-foot (1.8 to 3 m) dropoffs. These are best fished with a jig in full, 2- to 3-foot (60 to 90 cm) hops. Pike often take the jig as it drops.

5. SURFACE PLUG In late spring, fish topwater lures over weedbeds in the calm water of morning or late afternoon. Over the years, the combination of a slim minnow shape and propeller fuss has been most productive for me.

6. SPINNERBAIT Draw a spinnerbait past sprouting weeds and stop the retrieve for a three-count just as the bait approaches a possible hideout. Add a twist-tail or rubber-worm trailer for action and color contrast.

84

READ A PIKE BAY

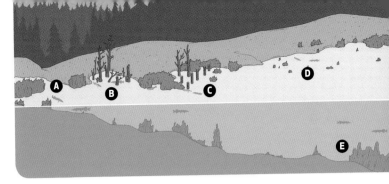

Mouths of swampy creeks (A) are starting points, but you'll catch more pike in the flats just offshore. Find one where the depth is 3 to 10 feet (1 to 3 m).

Ice-out pike gravitate to secondary coves that warm before the main bay. Pike might have spawned in the shallows or flooded timber (B) at the edges of such spots. Fish flats at the mouths of coves with in-line spinners.

Shoreline structures (C)— beaver dams, flooded timbers, downed trees—deserve a few casts. Work your way in, combing the flats in front with an in-line spinner.

As the spring sun warms the bay, weeds grow and pike orient to cover near dropoffs. Weedy points (D) make good fishing spots, as do midbay weed shoals. Search adjacent waters with an in-line spinner, flutter-retrieve a spoon, or stop and start a spinnerbait along the edges of the weeds. Deeper weedlines (E) near access to deep water are the last spots on the spring tour. Find the 6- to 10-foot (2 to 3 m) break. In general, pike over 10 pounds (4.5 kg) are the first to vacate the shallows for cooler water. This edge is the spot to try a jig-and-worm or to flutter-retrieve a spoon.

85

KNOW YOUR CHAIN PICKEREL

The smallest member of the Esox family, pickerel may not reach the sizes of their cousins the northern pike and muskie, but they are ferocious predators that fight hard. Found in ponds, lakes, bogs, creeks, and rivers from Maine to Florida, and inland to Wisconsin, they are less finicky than other Esox. Find a shallow, reed-filled cove, a cluster of lily pads, or a submerged tree and there's a good chance a pickerel is near. They ambush their prey, hovering in one spot, waiting for the perfect moment to strike. Catching one can be as simple as casting a live minnow under a bobber to likely holding areas, or as challenging as delicately presenting a streamer and watching them wake behind the fly before attacking. Pickerel are bony and not prized as table fare, but pickled they are a popular dish in certain

86 GO SHALLOW FOR POSTSPAWN MUSKIES

In early summer, postspawn muskies are ill-tempered and ravenous, prowling the shallows, looking for something to clobber. Make it your topwater lure. Here's how:

FIND THEM First, hit the shallow muck bays where the fish typically spawn. Next, target nearby points, downed trees, weed-and-rock transitions, cabbage, and sand-and-gravel shelves. Pay special attention to where wind is blowing into cover or structure. Shut down your boat motor about 75 yards (68 m) away from the structure, and use your trolling motor to sneak to within about 100 feet (30 m) of your target.

FOOL THEM Make a long cast. Bring a gurgling prop bait back with a steady retrieve, holding the rod tip low. Do the same with the dog-walker, but add repeated twitches that make the lure sashay from side to side. If you see a muskie following, don't stop the retrieve—speed it up. When the lure is about 10 feet (3 m) from the boat, release the reel's spool and make a figure L or 8. (If you're just searching, do an L. If you've had a follower, do a full figure 8 or two.)

LAND THEM The biggest mistake people make with topwater muskies is setting the hook too soon. Don't react to what you see, but wait until you feel the weight of the fish. Then come up and to one side with the rod tip—hard. Your drag should be screwed down so tight that you can hardly pull line out. Once you know you have a solid hookset, back off the drag to let the fish run. Then take your time and use a good muskie net to land your trophy.

87

STRIKE QUICK TO GET THAT MUSKIE

Most muskie hunters who send out live suckers are familiar with the quick-strike rig. This bait harness features two treble hooks connected by bite-proof steel wire. One hook is rigged in the bait's head and the other is near the tail to thwart short strikes. The only problem with the traditional quick-strike is that it doesn't do much to promote catch-and-release. That's easily fixed with a tiny rubber band and a flip of the bait. Rather than rig a sucker headfirst, plant one point of the lead hook in the tail. Then, using a rigging needle, thread a small rubber band through the bait's nostrils to create an anchor point for the second hook. Muskies will often attack headfirst, and with the treble seated in the rubber band, it can quickly break free upon the hookset, increasing the odds that the fish won't swallow the sucker and all that hardware. Not only will this help keep the muskie hooked just inside the mouth, but it will reduce the odds of the second hook snagging its face or gills, which can hinder a quick release.

88 DOG A MUSKIE

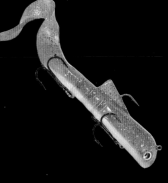

Before the Bull Dawg hit the scene in 1993, soft-plastic lures were not considered choice muskie baits. The Dawg changed that, earning a cult-like following for its productivity, versatility, and tough material that's capable of withstanding many strikes. Whether it is slow-crawled over the weeds, burned just subsurface, or jigged around structure, the nose-down falling orientation and high-vibration tail of this big-baitfish imitator turns trophy muskie heads with amazing consistency.

89 MESMERIZE A MUSKIE

The muskie carries a fearsome reputation for fickleness. The way to overcome this tendency is to finish every retrieve with the figure 8. Essentially, the figure 8 is a final enticement performed by the angler just before lifting the lure out of the water for another cast. To help visualize the concept, think of a roller coaster. As you move the lure from side to side, it also moves up and down. That 3-D action can really turn on a fish.

STEP 1 Cast and retrieve until there are 18 inches (46 cm) of line between the lure and the rod tip.

STEP 2 Dip rod tip 6 inches (15 cm) into water.

STEP 3 Draw a complete figure 8. The change in direction can incite a reluctant muskie to strike.

STEP 4 Keep in mind that a big muskie can come from below the lure, so you won't see the fish until it strikes.

90 FLIP A MUSKIE THE BIRD

To make the most of a duckling lure, start by scouting local waters and observing where ducks and their babies hang out most. Look in shallow bays and coves with an average depth of 10 feet (3 m) or less. Areas with timber or reeds that protrude above the surface are ideal, as the structure provides shelter for the birds.

The real trick to making a duckling lure look natural in the water is to make it behave like a baby bird that got separated from the family—which often happens on very windy days—and is frantically trying to find its mother. Achieving that action all comes down to some crafty, calculated rod work. Real baby ducks don't move in a straight line, and muskies know this.

Take advantage of this fact with a long cast, but thumb the spool before the bait lands. A live duckling weighs very little, so you want the lure to touch down with minimal splash, as would be the case with a duckling falling off a log or the bank.

Gently twitch the rod from side to side to make the lure move left and right. Don't overwork the rod, as ducklings don't move quickly or abruptly. After you've covered about 8 feet (24 m), give the lure a long pause.

Before you move the lure again, dip the rod tip in the water to pull the front of the lure downward. This makes the lure's bob more pronounced and helps mimic how a real duckling bobs, especially in a light chop.

91 KNOW YOUR MUSKELLUNGE

Better known as muskies, this big, bad predator fish is the largest member of the Esox family, which also includes northern pike and chain pickerel. Part of the appeal for dedicated muskie hunters is the skill and patience it takes to get hooked up to what's commonly referred to as the "fish of 10,000 casts." Muskie anglers are like a cult, and many of them have little interest in pursuing other species. Muskies can top 60 pounds (27 kg), but a fish that big may eat only once every other day. Be there at the right time with the right bait or lure or strike out. When a giant muskie does decide to feed, it usually wants a big meal. Many anglers consider live suckers the No. 1 live bait, but some swear by huge spinnerbaits, crankbaits, wooden jerkbaits, and monster jigs that can measure up to 14 inches (35 cm).

92 USE THE RIGHT CAT RIG

You don't need a lot of fancy gear to catch a cat. The two rigs that follow are killers. One tip for the bobber rig? Loop a tiny rubber band around the line for a bobber stop. This holds well and is easy to adjust.

BOBBER RIG Attach a bobber stop. Slide on a bead, 10-inch (25 cm) slip bobber, and ½-ounce (14 g) egg sinker. Tie to a No. 3 swivel with an 18-inch (46 cm), 25-pound (11 g) fluorocarbon leader and 8/0 octopus hook.

BOTTOM RIG Thread line through enough 2-ounce (57 g) egg sinkers to stay on bottom. Tie to a No. 5 barrel swivel; add a 12- to 24-inch (30 to 60 cm), 50-pound (23 kg) fluorocarbon leader and 8/0 octopus hook.

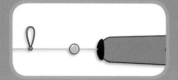

93 GO BULLISH ON BULLHEADS

These small catfish are usually easy to catch and also make for superb eating, which accounts for their huge popularity, especially in the Midwest. Rigging for bullheads is simple. Cover a size 4 to 1/0 hook tied to 6- to 8-pound (2.8 to 4.5 kg) test monofilament with a gob of small worms or a single nightcrawler. Add enough split shot about 18 inches (45 cm) above the hook to give adequate casting weight. Because bullheads are most active after dark, the action should increase after the sun goes down. Prop the rod in a forked stick and pay attention to your tackle so it doesn't get dragged in by a night-biting fish.

Bullheads have extraordinary senses of smell and taste, and those can help you catch them. Here's one way:

STEP 1 When you make your first cast into a bullhead pond, toss out your line at about a 60-degree angle to shore, then slowly reel your weighted worm back along the bottom.

STEP 2 Walk about 30 feet (9 m) along the shoreline and make another angled cast on a trajectory that would intersect your first, creating an imaginary X out in the water. Slowly drag the worm back once again.

STEP 3 Cast your bait to the X-spot intersection, sit down, and watch your line. The scent trails you've created should lead bullheads to the worm quickly. I've caught plenty by doing this, whenever bottom snags or weeds don't interfere.

94 CATCH A RESERVOIR CAT

The blue catfish, weighing in at 30 to 40 pounds (13 to 18 kg), can meet your monster-fish needs. Here's how to fish a reservoir and land a trophy that will bring tears to the eyes of any pro:

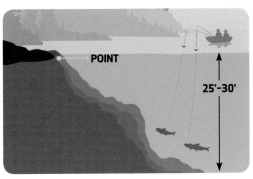

POINT

25'-30'

FLAT

CREEK CHANNEL

BOTTOM FEEDING This technique works well on a shallow flat that maintains a depth of 6 to 8 feet (2 to 2.5 m) for 50 yards (45 m) or more offshore before dropping sharply down to a creek or river channel. The biggest cats hover at the lip of the drop. Anchor your boat from the bow about 60 feet upwind of your target area and cast bottom rigs out over the transom. Set the rods in holders, put the reels in free spool, flip on the clickers, and wait. The bite is hottest when the wind blows baitfish up onto the flat.

SUSPENDED ANIMATION Mark suspended catfish with a depthfinder. (At 20- to 35-foot [6 to 10 m] depths, they often hold 5 to 10 feet [1.5 to 3 m] off the bottom.) Set your slip bobbers to keep the live baits 1 to 2 feet (30 to 60 cm) above the blues. Put your rigs out 25 to 75 yards (23 to 68 m) behind the boat. Place rods in holders and drift over fish. If there's little wind or current, use the electric trolling motor to get bobbers proper distance away from the boat. Once they hit the right distance, lock reel and slowly cruise around the area where the fish are holding.

95 FEED THE KITTY

Trophy blue catfish relish fresh baitfish—shad, skipjacks, and blueback herring. Use what's in the water you're fishing—most anglers catch their own with Sabiki rigs or cast nets.

LIVE BAIT Where there's little current, use a 6- to 9-inch (15 to 23 cm) live baitfish. Hook it through nostrils, or into the lower jaw and out

the nose, or under dorsal fin to keep bait lively. However, dorsal hooking lets it swim more freely, which can be an advantage in still water.

CUTBAIT This works well in current, which washes scent downstream, drawing catfish from long distances. Cut the fillets of a fresh skipjack herring into chunks.

96 GO BOBBING FOR CATS

Channel cats won't hesitate to rise to a bait, so an easy-to-cast slip-bobber rig is a perfect choice for bouncing shrimp or chicken livers in front of their noses. Work the rig around trees, fallen or standing, in 2 to 5 feet (.6 to 1.5 m) of water. In the morning or evening, float the rig along the edges of creek channels, making sure the bait rides 6 to 10 inches (15 to 25 cm) above the bottom. In high water, fish over flooded gravel roads.

FLOATS Slip bobbers come in a variety of shapes and sizes. Experiment with several to find one that casts comfortably. Look for a float that's user friendly and visible even in low light.

LINE The following components go onto the main line: a slip-bobber stop, a 2-mm plastic bead, the slip bobber, a 5-mm bead, and a small barrel swivel. Then finish the slip-bobber rig with an 18-inch (45 cm) braided leader, a No. 4 split shot, and a 1/0 circle hook.

BAIT Your first choice of bait should be a 3- to 4-inch (8 to 10 cm) cull or bait shrimp; the second is cutbait, such as shad, carp, or sucker. Paste-style stinkbaits can also produce strikes—especially in the late summer heat. Be sure to juice up your bait with your favorite choice of liquid attractant.

SKIN A TASTY CAT

Here's an old-school way to skin a midsize catfish.

SCORE IT Place a 3-foot-long (1 m) 2 x 6 (5 x 15 cm) board on a level waist-high surface, like a truck tailgate. Score the skin all the way around the head, just in front of the gill plates, then make a slit down the back.

NAIL IT Drive a 16-penny nail through the fish's skull to secure it to the board. Cut off its dorsal fin. Brace the board against your waist, grasp the skin with fish-skinning pliers, and pull it down to the tail and off.

GUT IT Remove the fish from the board. Grasping the head in one hand and body in the other, bend head sharply downward, breaking the spine. Now bend the body up and twist to separate head from body. Open the belly with your knife, remove the remaining viscera from the body cavity, and rinse well.

98 SCORE A MIDSUMMER STRIPER

The paradox of landlocked stripers is that they are big brawling fish that can reach 60 pounds (27 kg) and pull like a plow horse—but are also delicate, sensitive, and fussy. They function well in a very narrow temperature range: 55 to 65 degrees (13° to 18°C) is ideal. When temperatures soar, these fish are forced to go deep to find cooler water—but the deeper they go, the less dissolved oxygen becomes available to them. This causes a slow bite at best and a striper kill at worst. To score a midsummer striper, you need to target river-run reservoirs and the churning tailraces of power dams, where the water is cool, oxygen-rich, and loaded with big baitfish.

When a lake's temperature is in the 70s (21°C), stripers will suspend 20 to 30 feet (6 to 9 m) deep off main lake points, steep rock bluffs, and submerged standing timber along cavernous river channels. They'll bite best at sunup and sundown. Use stout baitcasting or spinning outfits to fish deep and vertical. Bait up with large gizzard shad (catch these in a cast net) or, where legal, 6- to 8-inch (15 to 20 cm) rainbow trout. Watch your bow-mounted sonar for suspending stripers and baitfish schools, then lower your baits to just above the level of the fish, moving slowly around the area with trolling motor until you contact active stripers.

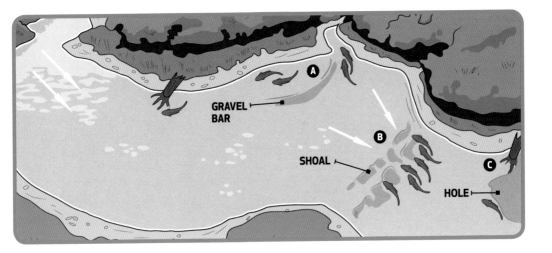

Labels on illustration:
A
GRAVEL BAR
B
SHOAL
C
HOLE

99 GIVE A DAM

When temperatures soar, move to water below a dam, where water is frigid and stripers get aggressive. Be there at first light, armed with beefy 7- to 8-foot (2 to 2.5 m) baitcasting outfits with wide-spool reels sporting heavy line (30- to 40-pound [13 to 18 kg]) mono or heavier braided line). Wolf packs of stripers cruise shallow shoals and gravel bars at daybreak (A), hitting schools of baitfish with percussive surface strikes. Start with a big, noisy muskie prop bait, retrieving it with loud rips and tranquil pauses. As fog burns off, switch to a quieter topwater glide bait, retrieving it slowly across the surface so the tail sashays back and forth, leaving a wake. By midmorning, move to 5- to 10-foot (1.5 to 3 m) holes adjacent to those shallow shoals and bars (B), casting a 10-inch (25 cm) soft jerkbait rigged with a treble stinger hook. Stripers hold tight to undercut banks and submerged trees (C); cast bait around these spots and skate it rapidly across the surface.

100 PULL BIG LIVE BAITS

In really hot weather, stripers pack into the upper reaches of cold-flowing rivers. Topwaters work early and late in the day, but in mid-afternoon a better approach is to pull big live baits—gizzard shad, skipjack herring, or rainbow trout—behind planer boards. You'll need an aerated circular shad tank to keep your bait frisky. Use 8-foot-long (2.4 m) medium-heavy baitcasting rods and big reels spooled with 40- to 50-pound (18 to 23 kg) mono or up to 30-pound (14 kg) braided line. Start upstream of your target and rig bait no more than 6 to 8 feet (2 to 2.5 m) behind the board to keep it from swimming into snaggy cover. Proceed slowly downstream under trolling-motor power, staying just ahead of the current so the board planes toward the shoreline. When your bait gets nervous, keep calm—a 40-pounder (18 kg) plastering a big shad on the surface sounds like a Buick falling off a bridge.

101 WORK THE INSHORE HIT LIST

The areas in and around inlets and bay systems are prime territory for predatory gamefish. No matter where you live, these 10 spots are going to hold gamefish in your local waters.

1. BEACH TROUGH Deep troughs close to the beach are gamefish magnets. Stripers, weakfish, tarpon, redfish, and pompano are a few species that cruise through looking for a meal. The easiest way to find troughs is to watch waves on the beach. If one breaks offshore and flattens suddenly, it often means the wave encountered a deep spot.

2. ISLAND CUT Tidal flow that gets squeezed between small islands will generally create a deep cut as it scours out the bottom. These cuts can create tremendous ambushing spots for all kinds of gamefish, though fish such as flounder, redfish, seatrout, and snook are some of the species known to use them most frequently.

3. CHANNEL CONFLUENCE Anywhere two deep channels come together in a bay system is a great place to look for fish, particularly bottom feeders such as flounder and black drum. As the tide moves, smaller forage species skirt along channel edges. Colliding currents where channels meet can disorient them, making them easy targets for gamefish.

4. INLET RIP In inlets, you'll often notice bulges, ripples, or standing waves on the surface, especially when tidal flow is at its peak speed. These disturbances are known as rips and are caused by structure or high spots on the bottom that force moving water to push up toward the surface.

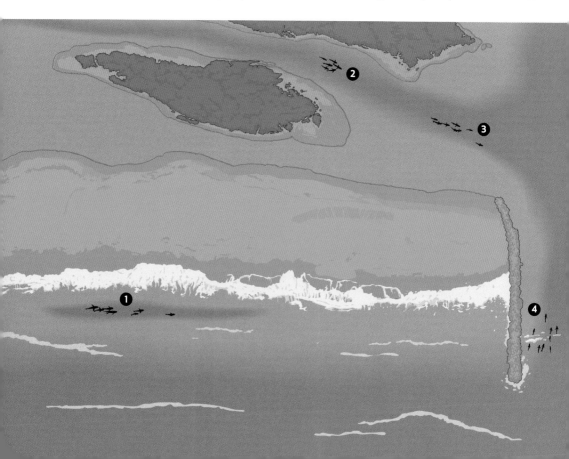

Gamefish stack up on the down-current side of whatever creates the rip, waiting for food to pass overhead.

5. INLET MOUTH When the tide is rushing out of a bay system, gamefish know to patrol the mouth of an inlet for a shot at an easy meal, as baitfish, shrimp, and other forage will be getting pulled into the ocean. Everything from tarpon to stripers, tuna to grouper will congregate here, and live baits or jigs worked near the bottom often produce best.

6. BUOYS It's always worth making a few casts around buoys and channel markers. These man-made structures provide a current break, and gamefish like seatrout and striped bass sometimes use that break to ambush bait. In the South, tripletail are notorious for hanging near markers and buoys. Cast a live or dead shrimp to the structure, and you'll know in short order if a tripletail is home.

7. JETTY TIP Whether the tide is pushing into an inlet or pulling out, jetty tips provide a current break where gamefish will wait for bait to get flushed past with the water flow. This is an excellent place to throw topwater lures that make lots of noise.

8. JETTY POCKET Incoming waves often scoop a deep depression along the beach where an inlet jetty meets sand. These pockets make terrific ambush points for everything from snook to sheepshead to striped bass. Gamefish will also work together to push a school of baitfish into a pocket so it can't escape. If you're prepared, neither can they.

9. TIDAL CREEK Even tidal creeks so small they are dry at low tide are worth fishing when the water's up. Small forage species know to use tidal creeks to get out of main channels at high tide. As the water falls, redfish, seatrout, flounder, and striped bass flock to the mouths of these creeks. Cast lures up into the creek and work them back into open water.

10. SHALLOW FLAT In the Southern and Gulf states, gamefish such as redfish, bonefish, tarpon, and permit are often found in skinny water, where they hunt for baitfish that are seeking refuge in the shallows and where they root for crabs and shrimp in the soft bottom. At the other end of the country, in the Northeast, gamefish such as striped bass and weakfish also hunt sand and mudflats during certain tidal stages, especially during marine worm hatches.

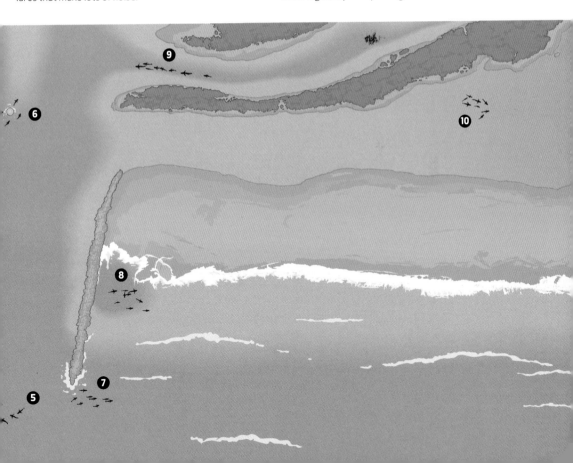

DANCE THE JIG

Diamond jigs are one of the simplest, yet effective, lures for catching bluefish and striped bass. These three methods will get you hooked up.

TOP SPEED Blues and stripers react best to baitfish fleeing quickly. When fish marks show up on your sounder in the middle of the water column, drop the jig all the way to the bottom and reel up as fast as you can. You don't have to jig the rod. When fish are keyed in to fast-moving bait, the hit will be a slam.

YO-YO When bait schools are really thick, below the surface of the water baitfish will be zipping in all directions, while injured baitfish flutter and fall to the bottom. To mimic a baitfish both fleeing and dying, drop to the bottom and lift the rod high into the air in a sharp stroke. As you lower the rod to jig again, quickly reel up the slack. This gives the jig a dart/fall action, and since you keep picking up slack, you'll work the entire water column until the jig is back on the surface.

SLOW DRAG When sand eels are the primary food source available, bass and bluefish hug the bottom because this species burrows in sand and mud. If you're marking patches of sand eels on the bottom in any location, let your jig touch down, pay out 20 extra feet (6 m) of line, and lock up the reel. Don't jig or crank; just let the lure drag across the bottom. It'll kick up sand or mud as it moves with the drifting boat, mimicking a fleeing sand eel. Bass and blues will slurp it right up.

103 BOB AN EEL

Live eels are one of the most effective baits for striped bass throughout their Eastern saltwater range of Maine to North Carolina. Though eels are traditionally fished weighted along the bottom, anglers in the Chesapeake Bay have perfected a different technique. Using an oversize round slip bobber, they'll suspend live eels at various depths throughout the water column, keeping one just off the bottom, one at midrange, and one just below the surface. Even in deeper water, a big bass will often rise to the shallowest eels, as their wiggle and dark silhouette stand out well against the back-lit surface and are irresistible to a cow striper. Though the method may have been developed in the Chesapeake, it works along any channel edge, hump, or rock pile that bass tend to frequent.

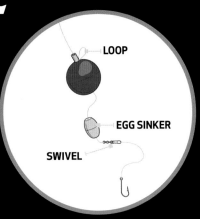

LOOP

EGG SINKER

SWIVEL

104 RIG AN EEL FOR STRIPERS

In August 2011, Connecticut angler Greg Myerson caught an 81.8-pound (37 kg) striped bass that trumped the former all-tackle world-record striper by nearly 3 pounds (1.3 kg). Myerson's fish ate a live eel, which is arguably one of the best striper baits ever. The problem with eels is they're expensive—about four bucks a pop. To be sure you get the maximum bang for those bucks, hook your eel through the top jaw and out one of its eyes. This lets the bait breathe better—and lets you return any uneaten eels to the live well for the next round.

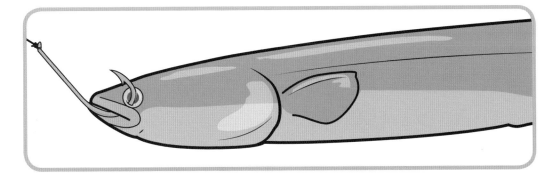

105 GO FROM POND TO BAYOU

Redfish and largemouth bass have a lot in common. They both live in fairly shallow water that's loaded with vegetation, they feed on a wide variety of prey, and they rely less on vision and more on sound and vibration when hunting for their next meal. With that in mind, it stands to reason that a lot of the lures designed to catch largemouth on lakes and farm ponds will put a serious hurt on redfish cruising through salty lagoons, backwaters, and marshes. Here are three bass lures you should never go on a redfish hunt without.

SPINNERBAIT These are great for redfish because the design allows them to run through weeds and grass without getting hung up, and the blade gives off flash and makes a thump reds can easily track, even when water is murky. Because they don't hang up easily, you can throw them into flooded reeds and marsh grass and drag them into open water. That's important because reds often hunt close to vegetation on shorelines.

CRANKBAIT One method that works well for bass anglers is bumping a crankbait off of stumps and rocks. This technique creates a knocking sound that gets the fish's attention and often prompts a strike. The same technique works for redfish whenever they are orienting to hard structure, such as oyster bars or rock jetties. Depending on the depth of the water, a shallow- or deep-diving crankbait might be in order.

CREATURE BAIT Creature baits look like aliens, and instead of resembling any specific forage species, they are designed to look like a combination of many and simply get a bass's attention. Because they can imitate everything from a crayfish to a lizard, they're bass killers. Put them in saltwater and they look like a crab or shrimp. Fished either on a jighead or a Carolina rig, these are deadly on reds that are grubbing the bottom.

106 GET THE GAFF

Knowing how to gaff a yellowfin tuna or albacore ranks next to opening a beer bottle with a knife blade on the manliness scale. Should you ever need to know, here's how to wield the gaff like a salty pro. Just make sure your gaff is sharpened. That's rule No. 1.

DEATH CIRCLE As the tuna tires, it will swim in circles (1) below the boat. The captain should keep the engines in gear so the fish swims parallel with the stern. Position yourself just ahead of the angler.

HEAD GAMES Hold the gaff at the rear and mid grips, and never take a wild swing. Keep the gaff point turned down and wait for a clear shot at the head (2) as the fish moves toward you.

POINT TAKEN Calmly but sharply pull the gaff into the fish's head (3) using both hands. Body shots will ruin the meat. Aim for the eyes. The ocular area is tough and offers a better hold for lifting the fish.

HIT THE DECK In one smooth motion, drag the fish over the gunwale (4). The boat's forward momentum should make this easier.

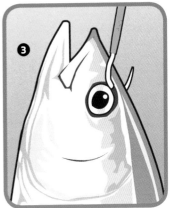

107 WORK A PENCIL POPPER

Pencil poppers are one of the most effective lures at imitating large baitfish splashing on the surface. Unlike standard short-body poppers, pencils take more than just a nudge of the rod tip to make a joyful noise. Follow these steps to whip a pencil like a pro.

RIP IT Pencil poppers are rear-weighted and will travel a mile. Using a 10- to 12-foot (3 to 3.5 m) soft-action surf rod, cast the popper as far as it will go (1). The greater the distance, the more time there is for the popper's loud splashing sound to draw in fish.

GRIP IT Bend your knees slightly and tuck the butt of the surf rod between your thighs (2). With your non-reeling hand, grab the rod blank 6 to 10 inches (15 to 25 cm) above the first guide. This position might feel a little bit awkward at first, but you'll get used to it.

WHIP IT Reel quickly as you whip the rod (3). The harder the rod flexes, the more forcefully the lure smacks and spits water. If a fish happens to strike, this position also puts the power at the center of your body for good balance and a solid hookset.

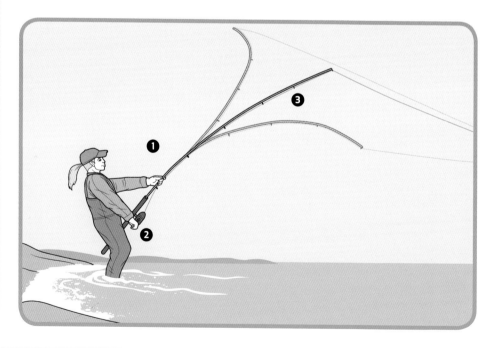

108 STING A FLATTIE

Fluke and flounder can be finicky and often need extra enticement to hit a jig or bait. One method that's grown popular with the advent of artificial baits is a bucktail stinger rig. Start by tying a three-way swivel to your main line. Using 6 inches (15 cm) of fluorocarbon, add a heavy bucktail jig (heavier than you think you need) to one eye of the swivel. Next, tie a 20-inch (50 cm) length of fluorocarbon to the other eye, with a 2/0 octopus hook on the trailing end. Thread a soft-plastic shrimp or mud minnow on the hook, drop the rig over a sandy or muddy bottom, and let it drag. It'll look like forage making a cloud, and when fish investigate, the trailing bait will be right in their face.

109 SNAP SOME RUBBER

Whether you're trolling for tuna in blue water or striped bass in the bay, rubber bands can catch you more fish and save you money. Send your trolling lure or bait out to the desired distance, loop a thick rubber band around the line (A), then loop the rubber band around the reel handle (B). This can get baits and lures a hair deeper, as your line will enter the water at a lower angle than it would coming straight off the rod tip. When a fish strikes, the rubber band snaps free of the reel handle and line, and you're clear to fight the fish.

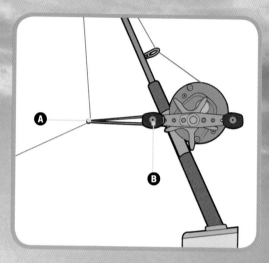

110

KNOW YOUR STRIPED BASS

Striped bass were historically native to the Atlantic Coast, with their primary range stretching from Maine to North Carolina. An anadromous fish—meaning they spawn in freshwater rivers but live in saltwater—stripers remain one of the most widely chased species in the Northeast. Given that they can hit the 80-pound mark and hunt close to shore, legions of anglers devote their springs, summers, and falls to pursuing these migratory gamefish. They can be caught by shore-bound anglers casting plugs and baits into the surf, or hooked by boaters dropping live baits and jigs within a few miles of land or in the bays. Stripers have also been stocked in many land-locked lakes throughout the country, as well as in the San Francisco Delta. No matter where you find stripers, they share one thing in common: They strike with a blow unlike any other species, and rip plenty of drag during the fight.

TACTICS

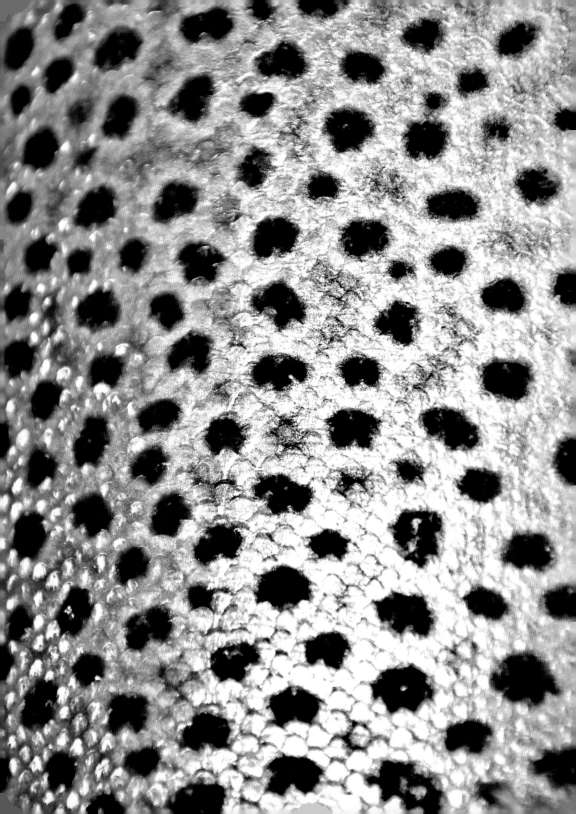

YOU'LL FIND THAT "IN THE ZONE"

gets thrown around in fishing as it does in other sports. For an angler, it's the feeling you get when everything starts to click. It's a sixth-sense intuition only anglers understand. You can almost predict that your lure, bait, or fly is about to get hit because you know that on this cast, on this drift, every element of the presentation is perfect. You don't just stumble into the zone. Getting there requires a working knowledge of the body of water you're fishing, an understanding of how fish behave, and the ability to decipher when you should change your approach. The best way to acquire those skills and instincts is through experience, though the tactics in this chapter will get you started.

111 BEAT THE WEEDS FOR FALL TROUT

Autumn can be a fabulous time to fish for trout, but you've got to learn to deal with the vegetation and change your tactics. After a summer's worth of growth, beds of aquatic plants spread in thick mats on the surface. Fish holding alongside or between islands of weeds or in shallow channels through the salad are supernaturally wary. Avoid wading if at all possible and stalk from the bank. Crouch. Creep. Crawl. Slither on your belly like a reptile. Do whatever it takes to get directly across from, or slightly below, the fish. Cast from a kneeling or sitting position.

Long, drag-free drifts are neither feasible nor necessary over shallow-lying fish holding around the weeds. A trout sees the surface of the water in a circular window centered above its head; the radius of the circle is roughly equal to the depth of the fish. A trout holding a foot (30 cm) down won't see your dry fly until it's 12 inches (30 cm) away. Drop the fly at the upstream edge of this window, laying your line directly atop any intervening vegetation. Let the fly float past the downstream edge of the window before picking it up—very quietly. If a hatch is in progress, it's likely Blue-Wing Olives.

Fish a size 18 Parachute BWO or emerger pattern. When nothing's hatching, choose a Parachute Adams or Crowe Beetle in the same size; small hook gaps are less likely to end up snagging on vegetation when you pick up the fly for another cast.

Bankside weeds and grasses reach their maximum height and droop low to the water, forming archlike tunnels that give trout shade and cover. To fish these prime runs, look for an entrance to the tunnel. Stay as far downstream from the opening as you can while still being able to pinpoint it with a cast. Drop a size 14 Elk Hair Caddis or ant pattern a few inches from the bank and let it snake down the tunnel. Your view may be screened, so strike at any disturbance.

If the overhanging vegetation is mostly long strands of grasses, you can take a brute-force approach: Use a pattern that is compact and bulletlike—a Dave's Hopper is good. Cast a tight loop to drive the fly through a thin spot in the curtain of grass. You may snag up a few times, but this tasty water is worth the trouble

Fall is terrestrial time on spring creeks, and the bugs are most active on warm days. Where you find open water or unobstructed banks that allow for a longer drift, flying-ant, beetle, and hopper patterns make excellent prospectors.

112 FIND A SECRET FISHING SPOT

Those little ponds in manicured neighborhoods and tucked behind strip malls can surprise you with bass, pickerel, crappies, and bluegills that are bigger and less pressured than those in the closest reservoir. You may never see such spots from main roads, so begin with some online sleuthing.

GO ONLINE Thanks to Google Maps, finding small bodies of water is easy. Start by entering your address into the search box and then zoom in or out until the scale in the bottom left corner of the map reads 1 inch = 500 feet (2.5 cm =152 m). Look for water in all directions. For hidden gems, focus on housing developments, shopping centers, and office complexes.

GO LOCAL Neighborhood ponds often existed long before the homes were built. Ponds in new developments are frequently stocked with gamefish to control mosquito populations and lily pads or milfoil to aerate the water. Heavy-commerce areas often have runoff retention basins (look by the back parking lots) or decorative ponds that hold fish. Of course, you can also find ponds hidden in the woods or a farmer's field, but fishing those may require knocking on doors. Not all of them will be accessible, of course, but that's all part of the hunt.

INVESTIGATE One pond, just 2 miles (3 k) from my home and ringed by backyards except at one corner, produced a 3-pound (1.4 km) bass and a few of its smaller cousins the first time I visited.

113 KNOW YOUR CRAPPIE

Prized as excellent table fare, both black and white crappies can be found throughout the country and are one of the scrappier members of the panfish family. With a larger mouth than sunfish and bluegills, crappies are more prone to attacking larger lures and baits, such as stickbaits and shiners. One of the most effective lures, however, is a small tube jig. Most anglers simply cast and retrieve tube jigs, but they can also be fished under a float or trolled. Crappies gravitate to areas with plenty of structure, with rockpiles, brushpiles, and weedlines being some of their favorites. Though during spring spawning crappies can be found in shallow water, most of the time fishing around deeper structure is a better bet. Hook a 3-pounder (1.4 kg), and you've got a giant, but the current world-record black and white crappies top the 4- and 5-pound (1.8 to 2.2 kg) mark.

114 AVOID DOUBLE-HAUL MISTAKES

Like most aspects of fly casting, the double haul is more about feel and timing than it is about power. To double-haul, you use your noncasting hand to pull the fly line away from the rod tip in an abrupt, well-timed burst—increasing resistance and flex in the rod—first on the back cast and then on the forward cast. By increasing that flex, you boost line speed. If you maintain a well-formed loop during your cast, that added energy translates to distance. The trick is to avoid these three common mistakes.

TOO MUCH LINE You need to feel what you're doing in order to get your timing down, and that's hard to do with 60 feet (18 m) of line flying overhead. Start short, with maybe 20 feet (6 m) of line. Pull the line on your back cast, feel the resistance, and let the line spring back through the guides (sliding through your fingers so you can pinch it again). Give it another tug on the forward cast, release, and shoot the cast.

Don't try long casts until you get the groove with short ones.

NOT GIVING THE LINE BACK TO THE ROD You're sunk if your cast ends up with your line hand down by your hip pocket, 3 feet (1 m) away from your casting hand, with dead line flapping in between. All the energy is lost. Your hands should spring apart and come together like you're playing an accordion. If necessary, tie your wrists together with a 20-inch (50 cm) piece of string.

HOLDING ON When it's time to let fly with that cast, let go of the line! Haul on the back cast, haul on the forward cast, feel the flex, and when your loop gets ahead of your rod tip, let go of the line as if you're shooting a slingshot through the guides on your rod. Hanging on kills the cast. You'll soon learn how to gently release and regather the line with your fingertips as you're double-hauling.

115

UNSTICK YOURSELF

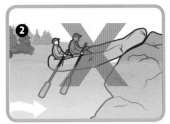

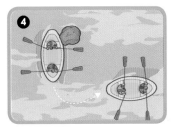

If you find yourself stuck against a rock (1), the worst thing you can do is recoil. Leaning away from the rock shifts weight upstream, forcing that side of the boat or raft to dip deeper in the current (2) and upping your odds of sliding up onto the rock and getting pinned there. If you hit a rock, it's typically best to lean into the rock (3) so water pressure can buoy the boat and help spin you off to the side.

The oarsman can help spin the boat free by pulling back on the upstream oar if the rock is in front of the center point of the boat (4) or by pushing forward if the rock is behind the center point.

116

KNOW YOUR CUTTHROAT TROUT

Though cutthroat trout are stocked in some areas of the country, they are, by and large, found only in their native range in the Rocky Mountains from Washington to parts of Arizona and New Mexico. They get their name from the distinct red or orange slash mark below their bottom jaw. Unlike brown and rainbow trout, cutthroat trout are broken up into several subspecies, with Yellowstone cutthroats and West Slope cutthroats being the most widespread and available. Stunningly beautiful, cutthroats inhabit everything from high mountain lakes to tiny mountain trickles to major river systems. They are willing eaters that will hit many small lures and natural baits, but they are arguably most prized by flyfishermen who prefer dry flies. Even when an insect hatch is not occurring, cutthroats are quick to rise to attractor patterns, such as a Stimulator.

117 MASTER 8 MINNOW TRICKS FOR TROUT

If you want to hook a trout with spots as big as dimes, you're going to have to offer it a proper meal, not just a little snack. To that end try one or more of these eight natural and artificial approaches to matching live minnows—and you might just hook the biggest fish in the pool.

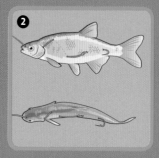

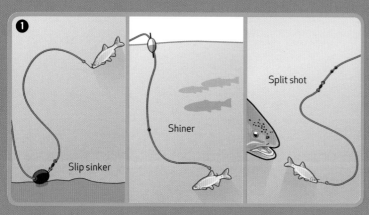

1. LIVE MINNOW For a shore-fishing rig, thread a ³⁄₄-ounce (21 g) slip sinker on the line above a swivel. On the bottom of the swivel, tie a 2-foot (60 cm) section of 6-pound (2.75 kg) test fluorocarbon and a No. 4 hook. Add a 3- to 4-inch (7.6 to 10 cm) shiner hooked through the lips. Tie a rubber band in an overhand knot around the base of the rod. After casting, open the bail and tuck a loop of line beneath the rubber band. You can prop the rod in a forked stick, because the minnow isn't strong enough to pull out the loop, and such little resistance won't cause a trout to drop the bait as it runs with it. If snags litter the bottom, a shiner beneath a bobber is a better choice. Unlike warmwater fish that cruise just off the bottom, salmonids often swim through the mid-depths. Use the smallest float that will support the shiner and a single split shot. Hook the 3- to 4-inch (7.6 to 10 cm) minnow lightly through the back. To fish live shiners from a boat, replace the slip sinker with split shot. Drift the shore in an area where you can see the bottom on one side of the boat but not on the other.

2. SEWN MINNOW Push a No. 4 hook down through the nasal vent of the shiner and out the bottom of the throat. Then bring the hook down through the upper back all the way through the bottom of the fish. Slip the hook beneath the skin on its side and slowly tighten. The body should curve enough to make the bait turn and flip in the water (too much curve will make it spin). A very slow stop-and-start retrieve with the occasional twitch is often the best. Fish a sewn minnow in a stream's deep, slow water. Cast upstream and roll the bait along the bottom; add whatever split shot you need to get it down. In a boat, drift and cast toward the shore, working from the shallow into the deep. When the bait reaches the dropoff, stop the retrieve, and let it flip and flop and glide to the bottom.

3. RIGGED MINNOW This setup retains the natural form of the baitfish and benefits from a quicker, more aggressive retrieve. It works particularly well once the water begins to warm. Keep the minnow alive as long as possible by hooking the single main No. 6 hook through the nasal vent and the stinger hook through the skin just below and behind the dorsal fin. Make the rig by tying the stinger hook to the tag end of a clinch knot in a 2-foot, 6-pound (60 cm, 2.7 kg) fluorocarbon leader. Two inches (5 cm) between the main hook and a size 12 to 14 treble is the proper distance. Cast above obstructions such as logjams and boulders and

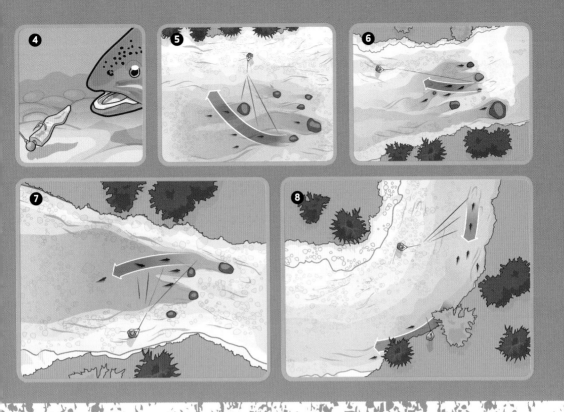

twitch it back with the flow, working crosscurrent, pausing when the minnow is within striking distance of the hideout. This is where the wriggle of a live shiner pays off.

4. CUTBAIT Cutbait can be still-fished on the bottom in pools, but an even better method is to hook it to a small jighead and drop it over a steep bank, jiggling and twitching it as it falls to the bottom, where you let it rest. Old-timers used a chub tail when there were so many creek chubs that they gobbled down the worm before the brook trout could get to it. The chub tail also tended to attract the biggest trout in a pool. The same strategy can be effective today. A good spot in the high water of spring is the first big pool of a feeder creek upstream from the main river.

5. STICKBAIT Minnow imitators are best as water starts to drop. They run through very shallow water, and you can control depth by retrieval speed or model choice, which makes them ideal for river fishing. Smaller suspending lures are excellent big-river stickbaits. They hold at a depth rather than popping to the surface once you stop reeling. Cast upstream and work the stickbait crosscurrent. It should wobble slowly when it gets to the target.

6. SPINNER The trick to catching big trout with spinners is to turn and face the flow so the lure simulates a minnow moving along the bottom. Cast a spinner as far upstream as possible and reel just fast enough to keep ahead of the current. The long heavy blade will tick off the rocks. Try to match the blade to the stain of the water—silver in clear, gold in tannin. As the waters recede, fish the transition line along the dropoff to the main river channel.

7. STREAMER The key to presenting a streamer is to work it crosswise to the current so its full profile is visible to trout. Cast farther upstream than you think you should, giving the streamer time to sink. Use a floating line, which makes mending possible and lets you keep the streamer broadside. Use a bucktail in the fastest water, feathers in a moderate current, and a marabou in slow water.

8. SPOON Flutter along dropoffs in lakes, making the spoon imitate a baitfish trying to right itself. In early-season rivers, stand over deep pools and jig a Little Cleo along undercut banks. Later in spring, cast upstream and work back with the current, letting the spoon flutter into the head of the pool.

118 PLAY TO A SURFACE-FEEDING TROUT

Watching trout rise from a vantage point on the riverbank will tell you where to cast. But by taking an even closer look and noting how those trout are rising, you can also glean exactly what type of fly to throw at them—especially when many different bugs are flying in the air. Here's what to look for.

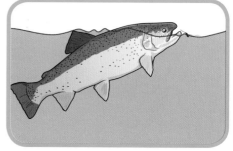

THE SIP A very subtle dimple appears in the water, and only the nose of the trout surfaces. This means the fish are either sipping midges or eating spent mayfly spinners.

THE SLURP If you see more pronounced "beaks" on the surface, fish are dialed in on a hatch—likely mayfly duns. When the fish are really chopping, try a crippled fly variation.

THE SPLASH A sudden, explosive pop with some splash says that the trout are on moving targets, like skittering caddisflies. Tie on a caddis pattern and don't be afraid to give it a twitch.

THE BOIL When you see disturbed water but no faces—only a dorsal fin and maybe a tail—that's the sign that fish are eating emergers before they reach the surface.

119

DROP RIGHT IN

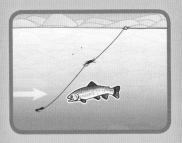

Fishing two flies—an old method that has enjoyed a renaissance in recent years—lets you turn fluctuating water levels into an opportunity. The following fly rigs allow you to adjust your presentation to any level. With both rigs, strikes often come at the end of the drift. Drag causes the dropper to rise, simulating a hatching nymph and triggering a strike. When you're about to give up on the drift, be ready.

HIGH-WATER RIG In more torrential waters, attach an indicator at the butt of a 3X leader. Tie a size 8 weighted stonefly nymph to the end of the leader. On the hook bend, tie 2 feet (60 cm) of 4X tippet with an improved clinch knot. At the terminal end, tie on a size 12 Hare's Ear or a size 12 Sparkle Pupa. The leader should be 1 to 2 feet (30 to 60 cm) longer than the water is deep, depending on the current speed. Then, cast upstream and present the nymphs drag-free. When a fish takes, the indicator will twitch, lurch, or sometimes just stop.

LOW-WATER After water levels fall, begin with a size 12 elk hair caddis. On the hook bend, tie 3 feet (1 m) of 4X or 5X tippet with an improved clinch knot. At the other end, tie on a size 14 Caddis Pupa or a size 16 or 18 Beadhead Pheasant Tail. Cast upstream and present the flies drag-free. Set the hook if the dry fly twitches or disappears.

120

KNOW YOUR BROWN TROUT

While brown trout can be found in almost every state in the Union, many anglers don't realize this common species is not native to the United States. All brown trout, from the wild stream-bred fish in the American West to those grown in East Coast hatcheries, are descendants of either the Loch Levin strain from Scotland or those originally native to the forests of Germany. Smaller brown trout in streams, rivers, and lakes can be quite ravenous, readily attacking stickbaits, spinners, and a wide variety of flies. Jumbo browns in the 24- to 30-inch (60 to 75 cm) range, particularly those that live in rivers, are often considered "wise" and wary, holing up under gnarly logjams and in the deepest pools, where they feed only once or twice a day. Browns this size will eat anything from a mouse swimming across the surface to a trout half their own body length.

121 FISH WITH YOUR EYES

"How in the world did you see that?" is a refrain fishing guides often hear. Spotting fish before you cast can dramatically increase your odds of hooking up. It doesn't require Superman vision or a carrot-rich diet to start sighting fish. Follow these rules, and you'll see your way to instant gratification on the water.

DISCARD DISTRACTIONS
The sooner an angler can weed out distractions like wind, ripples, and bird shadows, the sooner he can identify the position of feeding fish.

LOOK AHEAD Any fish that are upstream of you facing the current can't see you, so it's important to keep an eye ahead of you if you don't see any fish closer to your feet.

ZERO IN Instead of searching the entire area, focus on one small zone at a time. Tunnel vision is actually a good thing when you're contemplating where to place that next cast.

SEARCH FOR THE SUBTLE
Look for reflections, shapes, and shadows that might reveal a fish. A tail or a nose can be all you need to identify a target.

WATCH THE SURFACE
The motion of schooling fish reveals their locations. If a noticeable disturbance occurs as you stare at a smooth water surface, keep looking. Flashes of tails often follow in spots where you first see ripples.

GET THE EYES Polarized sunglasses are a must. You can't see fish without them. Try to position yourself so the sun makes a spotlight on the water, and wear the right color lenses for the conditions.

SPOT INCONSISTENCIES
Whether you're seeking out bedded bass or trout holding in a run, identify unusual marks in the water. Color shades, shadows, and motion can tip you off to a lurking fish.

LOOK THROUGH Practice looking through the water column—not fixing your gaze on the surface or the bottom. Doing this lets you observe motion and subtle color changes that pinpoint fish.

122 HOOK MORE RISING FISH

Instead of setting the hook when you see a fish take your fly, wait until you see your leader move. Fish often roll to sink a fly and then take it on a second pass. Giving yourself that extra moment will allow you to confirm that you have a solid hit and not a passing swipe.

123

KNOW YOUR FLATHEAD CATFISH

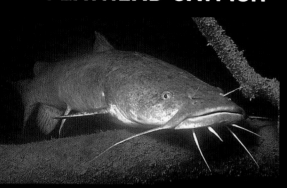

When you hear about a noodler wiggling his fingers in a submerged rockpile and ripping out a 100-pound (45 kg) catfish with his bare hands, that catfish is most likely a flathead. Native to the lakes and rivers stretching north and south from Mexico to North Dakota and east and west from the Appalachian Mountains to Arizona, flatheads are voracious predators and highly territorial. For those not brave enough to let a big flathead clamp down on their extremities, live bluegills or shad are preferred baits, and nighttime is often the right time to connect with these brutes. Flatheads thrive in murky, muddy water—look for them in soft-bottom channels, around rocky ledges, and in backwater holes and eddies that create a good spot for a big cat to lie in ambush, waiting for its next meal.

124

DRIFT AND DREDGE

A drifting canoe is a superb platform from which to dredge deep water. Cast straight across the current for the deepest drifts or slightly downstream so the lure swings across the current, then turns toward the boat. Fish often strike right when it changes direction. To slow your drift, turn the canoe around and float backward. Take turns fishing with your paddling partner, because the stern paddler has to control the speed with occasional paddle strokes. This is a great way to fish long pools. Another option is to rig a "drag chain." Attach a length of heavy chain to your anchor rope—remove the anchor first, of course—and drag it behind the boat. Covering the chain with a bicycle-tire inner tube dampens the noise from any contact with the hull and bottom.

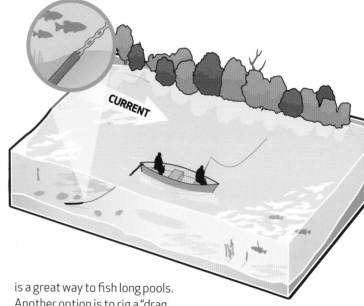

CURRENT

125 GET THE DROP ON BASS

Done right, a drop-shot rig can be irresistible to even picky fish. The key is the rate at which it sinks; soft-plastic bait should fall flat through the water, not dive nose-down. To accomplish this, try a 1/32-ounce (1 g) split shot. During the spawn and postspawn, shorten the space between the bait and the tag end, where you hang the split shot, to 4 inches (10 cm) or less (A). By cutting the tag end down, you minimize the problem of tangling around structures.

Bass will often attack the soft plastic as it falls through the water. If the bait hits the bottom without a strike, shake the rod to give the worm some enticing action. After a few shakes, gently retrieve the bait, then cast to your next target. Concentrate on tempting shallow-water largemouths around docks, near deadfall, and adjacent to vegetation (B). Also, try to intercept postspawn lunkers on shelves adjacent to flats (C).

Try fishing a 7-foot (2 m) medium-action spinning rod and a spinning reel spooled with green fluorocarbon line. In open water, use 6-pound (2.75 kg) line; near structure, use an 8- to 10-pound (3.6 to 4.5 kg) line. For the rig, use a 7-inch (18 cm) worm in triple margarita, a 4/0 Gamakatsu EWG hook, and one 1/32-ounce (1 g) split shot. Work at close range, pitching around tree limbs, docks, and so forth.

Because this rig requires light line, target a spot close to where you think bass are and entice them away from cover. The natural action of the gliding drop-shot bait will make this possible.

126 PULL BASS FROM BENEATH THE BOARDS

Bass like docks because they provide shelter and a steady supply of baitfish. But how largemouths relate to docks in spring depends on the spawning stage. On any given lake, you'll find bass in all three modes: prespawn, spawn, and postspawn. Here's how to fish docks no matter which stage the fish are in.

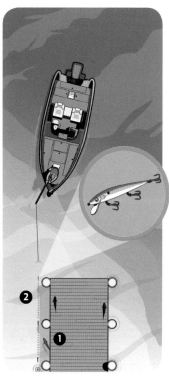

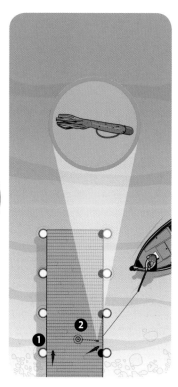

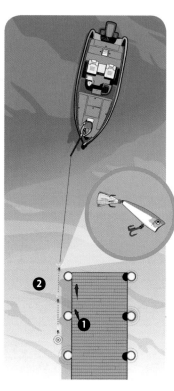

PRESPAWN Concentrate on docks off spawning areas where there is quick access to deeper water, such as those near main-lake points, secondary points, and steep banks. Work a shad-color suspending jerkbait parallel to the outer edges of the docks, where prespawn bass tend to hold (1). Let bait hover for 3 seconds between twitches (2). Another excellent choice is a ¼- to ½-ounce (7 to 14 g) black-and-blue skirted jig matched with a pork-rind trailer. Swim it a few feet beneath the surface along the dock edges to imitate a bluegill. Or hop it along the bottom to mimic a crayfish.

SPAWN Spawning bass gravitate to docks in shallow water, typically to the pilings at the near shore end (1). They also often spawn beneath the walkway connecting floating docks to shore. Here, use a 4- or 4½-inch (10 to 11 cm) Texas-rigged tube, and peg a ³/16- to ⁵/16-ounce (5 to 9 g) bullet sinker against the lure to keep it from sliding up the line. Flipping, pitching, or skipping the lure far under the dock will produce the most strikes (2). Though it takes time to master the flip, the cleaner the presentation, the more strikes you'll draw, as the first drop often counts most.

POSTSPAWN As the spawning period wanes, you can find excellent topwater action around docks. Before heading back toward deep water, postspawn bass may continue to hold near shallow docks for a few days. They tend to suspend under a dock's outside edges (1) and will nail a topwater popper worked past them (2). The window of opportunity can be relatively short for postspawn stragglers, as their willingness to stay will depend largely on the amount of forage species around the dock. However, these bass can offer some of the most exciting fishing of the year.

127

KEEP ON THE GRASS

Although smallmouth bass often hang out near rocks and gravel, they also feel at home in aquatic vegetation, especially right after the spawn, when smallies gravitate to prey-rich weedbeds to fatten up before migrating to their summer haunts. Look for greenery on points, humps, and the edges of dropoffs in 3 to 8 feet (1 to 2.5 m) of water (or a little deeper in clear lakes). The bass will relate to the outside edges of the weeds, as well as the lanes and pockets that make ideal ambush zones. Use any of these tactics to pluck bass from the grass.

DANCE A TOPWATER BAIT, a proven winner for this kind of fishing. Make long casts with a 7-foot (2 m) medium-heavy baitcasting rod, a high-speed reel, and 15-pound (7 kg) line. Work that popper or spook all of the way back to the boat and steel yourself for some explosive strikes.

BURN A SPINNERBAIT over the grass to trigger jolting reflex strikes. Use the same baitcasting outfit as at left and tie on a ½ - to ¾-ounce (7 to 21 g) chartreuse spinnerbait rigged with slightly undersize double-willow chartreuse blades, which will keep the bait from rolling.

SWIM A TUBE on 10-pound (4.5 kg) line with a 6½-foot (2 m) medium-heavy spinning outfit. Slide a ¹⁄₁₆-ounce (1.75 g), exposed-hook jig into a 3½-inch (9 cm) root beer–green flake tube. Cast out and work bait in very slowly. Done right, the lure seems to hover over the grass and coaxes bites even from tentative bass.

WORK A JERKBAIT with a jerk-jerk-pause-jerk-pause cadence. Use 10-pound (4.5 kg) line with a 6-foot (1.8 m) medium-action baitcasting or spinning rod, which mitigates the fatigue you feel in your wrists when you fish jerkbaits with heavier tackle. Strikes come during the brief pauses, and there won't be any guesswork.

128

KNOW YOUR SMALLMOUTH BASS

Much like largemouth bass, smallmouths can be fooled into eating anything from live bait to flies to just about every style of artificial lure available. What sets them apart, however, is their scrappy nature. Smallmouths are known for the bulldog fighting abilities that trump their largemouth cousins. Hook a smallmouth in a deep lake, and it's going to make every effort to swim to the bottom and snap your line. Hook one in a swift, rocky river, and it will try to find a boulder to wrap around and bust you off. Though these fish can be found throughout the United States in many types of water, their preferred habitat includes a combination of cooler water, rocky structure, and current, making them much more prevalent in rivers, particularly in the Northeast and Northwest, than largemouth bass.

129 TAKE IT TO THE SLOPES

Steep structures allow sluggish early-spring bass to make major depth changes without swimming long distances.

ROCK BLUFFS These structures consistently produce prespawn bass, and because the rock walls are typically apparent above the shoreline, they're easy to locate. Look for bass to suspend along the face of bluffs, where they'll make quick vertical movements to pick off baitfish.

STANDING TIMBER In spring, target emergent timber that lines the edges of major creek runs, rather than submerged timber along very deep river channels. Bass will suspend around the trees, warming themselves in the sun, and then move into the shade to ambush prey.

SUBMERGED HUMPS Avoid the tops of these structures in spring. Use your graph to pinpoint the side or end with the sharpest slope.

RETAINING WALLS In lakes that have a good deal of residential development on or around them, wood pilings or concrete blocks often line the banks to prevent erosion. Bass readily cruise these vertical walls looking for shad and crayfish. When they're not feeding, they'll drop back and suspend off the structure.

45-DEGREE BANKS These banks are far from vertical, but they slope into deep water fairly quickly and often have small, steep ledges on them that hold bass. A suspending jerkbait will work here; fish it with slow twitches.

130 CAST THE CRANKS OF SPRING

When it comes to hooking coldwater bass in early spring, you can't beat crankbaits. These lures swim with a tight wiggle that appeals to lethargic bass in water below 50 degrees (10°C). Here are four varieties to keep in your tackle box.

COFFIN BILLS A crankbait with a coffin bill fends off snags. A ½-ounce (14 g) lure is heavy enough to cast accurately to windfalls and other snaggy cover. Crank slowly as it comes through the structure, and pause every time it pops over a limb.

LIPLESS RATTLERS Most of these sinking, hard-vibrating crankbaits have noisy rattles. Slow-roll them over submerged grass 5 to 10 feet (1.5 to 3 m) deep. Most strikes are going to happen after you snap the rattler through a strand of the grass.

FLAT DIVERS These will descend to 8 feet and have nearly neutral buoyancy. They're ideal for cranking banks that slope into the water at a 45-degree angle. Target pea gravel to basketball-size chunk rock at the mouths of spawning coves. Tick the bottom with a slow to medium-slow retrieve. Go with a shad or crawfish color.

THIN MINNOWS The subtle roll and twitch tempts bites when sluggish bass shun more active lures. Run it over 45-degree-angle banks and secondary points. Also, slowly retrieve the lure parallel to each side of a dock to pull bass from beneath. An occasional stop-and-go cadence can make a huge difference.

131 KNOCK ON WOOD

Stumps may be a great place to lose lures, but they're also baitfish magnets, and hungry bass traveling to and from spawning beds pause beneath their gnarled roots to rest and feed. Pay attention to the spawning cycle to hit the stumps most likely to hold big bass.

PRESPAWN Stumps along channel bends and junctures in the lake hold bass before they start for spawning areas. Probe with a 1/2-ounce (14 g) black-and-blue jig-and-pig. In clear water, hover a jerkbait or slowly retrieve a subtle-action crankbait over them.

TRANSITION As bass move into tributaries to spawning grounds, they pause to rest and feed. Bump stumps with a jig-and-pig, a crawdad-color crankbait, or a 6-inch (15 cm) junebug-colored lizard Carolina-rigged.

STAGECRAFT Before the spawn, bass stage in stump rows along the edges of shallow channels high in the arms of tributaries. Tap a jig-and-pig or the lip of a fat shallow-running crankbait in a crawdad color off the tops.

BEDTIME In old reservoirs, where upstream shallows are covered in soft silt, spawning bass will lay their eggs on the hard surfaces of stumps and their roots. Flip a black neon and junebug–colored Texas-rigged tube or lizard on top of a stump and let it lie there, twitching. Don't retrieve too quickly.

STUMPING FOR STRIKES A good way to attract bass that may not otherwise see your bait is to cast close enough to a stump for your lure or sinker to bang against it. If you're using a heavy jig or plastic bait, don't retrieve it too quickly.

THE MORNING AFTER If you found stumps holding bass during the prespawn, try them again once the fish leave their beds.

132 THROW A ONE-TWO BASS PUNCH

There's a variety of reasons that a bass might strike at your lure and end up missing it completely. Disappointing as this is in the moment, at least a miss tells you where the fish are and that they're in an aggressive mood. The key to catching fish that miss is using a totally different lure to draw an impulse strike.

SPINNERBAIT TO LIGHT TUBE JIG Flashing blades and vibration attracted the bass. Follow with a tube that sinks slowly. Snap the tube with your rod to create multiple falls, mimicking injured forage.

FLOATING FROG TO SMALL JIG Bass often miss frogs if they don't actually see them, but only hear the frog when it lands somewhere in heavy vegetation. In this situation, use a finesse jig, which falls slowly and is easy to see. In more open water, slight twitching makes the jig deadly.

TOPWATER BUZZBAIT TO PLASTIC WORM The buzzbait will be what triggered the surface strike. Follow with a worm rigged weightless and wacky-style so it produces a vibrating fall that hovers in front of the fish.

133

KNOW YOUR YELLOW PERCH

With the exception of the Great Lakes, where recreational anglers and large charter boats that hold more than 30 people target perch year-round, open-water fishing is not the primary way people in America catch perch; ice fishing for perch is much more popular. Yellow perch remain highly aggressive all winter long and are often easier to coax into feeding during the cold season than species such as crappies and bluegills. The short rods necessary for ice fishing are also perfectly suited to getting the maximum fight out of a scrappy perch. Tiny soft-plastic jigs, little spoons, and small live minnows or maggots are popular baits and lures for targeting perch through the ice. In open water, these fish will take a swing at a number of lures, including small in-line spinners and slender stickbaits

134 LEARN DEEP SECRETS

Two places to consistently find active bass when it's hot are long, sloping points that reach far offshore before dropping off, and the lips of creek and river channels (ledges), especially on outside bends and channel junctures.

Start by idling around the main lake while viewing your depthfinder. Normally, you'll see suspended fish, which are typically inactive at a certain depth, often about 14 feet (4 m) or so. Remember that number once you determine it, because that's where you're going to find feeding bass on points and ledges throughout the lake.

DEEP CRANKING Comb the points and ledges with a ½- to 1-ounce (14 to 28 g) long-billed shad-pattern crankbait that will run deep enough to tap the bottom at the depth you're fishing. Use a 7-foot (2 m) medium-action baitcasting rod and 8-pound (3.6 kg) line, and make long casts to get your bait to its maximum depth. These crankbaits work best at 18 (5.4 m) feet or less.

CAROLINA RIGGING For fishing in waters down to 30 feet (9 m) or more, it's hard to beat a Carolina rig, which casts far, sinks fast, and stays in the strike zone throughout the retrieve. Casting these rigs calls for a heavy-action 7- to 7½-foot (2 to 2.3 m) baitcasting outfit. Use a 4-inch (10 cm) French-fry worm Texas-rigged on a 3/0 worm hook. Watermelon and pumpkinseed are proven summertime colors.

HEAVY JIGGING If you're after big bass, cast a ½- to ¾-ounce (14 to 21 g) weedless jig dressed with a plastic craw, using a 7-foot (2 m) medium-heavy baitcasting rod and 12-pound (5.4 kg) line. Go with crawdad colors in clear water and black-and-blue in stained water. After casting, jump the jig off the bottom with long sweeps of the rod, then let it swing back to the bottom while you hold the rod tip high. This bait isn't apt to catch as many fish as the subtler Carolina rig, but the jig's big profile will trigger strikes from some of the lake's heftiest bass.

135

TAKE THE LONG SHOT

THE SPOT Black crappies begin spawning when the water hits 60 degrees (15°C), usually in 3 to 10 feet (1 to 3 m) of water over a sand or gravel bottom. Points near creek channels at the mouths of bays are excellent places to start the hunt. The fish may hold anywhere from the end of the point to just inside the bay, and the more points you hit, the more fish you'll catch.

THE LURES A 2-inch (5 cm) curly-tailed grub on a ⅛-ounce (3.5 g) jighead is a traditional search bait, but small swimbaits and tiny diving crankbaits are equally effective and have actions fish may not see as often. Keep one of each rigged on your boat deck for quick presentation changes without retying. In clear water, light colors like chartreuse and white are top producers.

THE GEAR Light-action spinning rods measuring 6½ to 7 feet (2 m) are ideal for making long casts with small lures. A crappie's mouth is soft, so choose a rod with a slow tip to keep hooks from pulling free during the set and

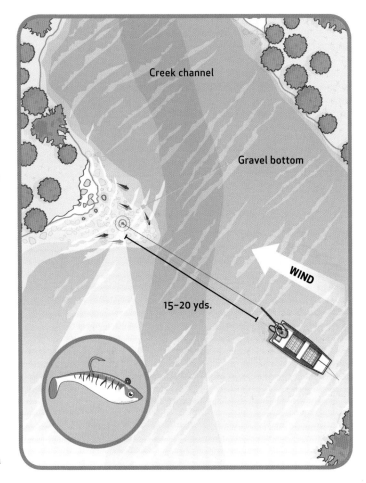

Creek channel

Gravel bottom

WIND

15–20 yds.

fight. Small-diameter braided line helps lengthen cast and is sensitive enough to detect subtle bites at a distance.

THE METHOD Keep your boat at least 15 to 20 yards (13 to 27 m) away from the point. Breezy days tend to be more productive, as a chop on the water generally makes fish active and helps break up your shadow and reflection. Stay upwind of the point and fan

cast across it, working the lure with a slow, steady retrieve. In clear cool water, a crappie's strike may be quick and light, so set the hook immediately on even the slightest bump. When you catch one fish, drop anchor and spend at least a half hour covering the point with casts. It's common for action to ebb and flow, but rest assured: In spring, if you've found one crappie, more are holding in the same location.

136 CATCH WALLEYES SIX WAYS

Take to the lake in your boat and try one or all of these walleye pro techniques.

STAY BOLD After a cold front shuts down the bite, most anglers go to lighter tackle and slower presentations. Try a contrary approach, using bigger lures and erratic retrieves to provoke strikes. Rip a jigging spoon, as this classic ice-fishing lure can fire up lethargic open-water walleyes. Choose a ¼- to ½-ounce (7 to 14 g) model and cast to the edges of weedbeds, timber, or rocky structure. Wait for the lure to flutter to the bottom, then jerk the rod tip to rip the spoon toward the boat. Let it sink and repeat.

GET ON BOARD For eliciting bites from walleyes, planer boards are unparalleled—but they certainly don't do any good if you miss those strikes. When you troll a crawler harness beneath a board, add a flag strike indicator. The flag signals any slight change of the planer's action. Also, because short-striking walleyes often nip the bait below the terminal hook on a standard harness, use a No. 10 light-wire treble at the very end of the crawler to nab sneaky bait stealers.

DO THE SLIDE Add slider rigs to your trolling setup. These are basically droppers attached to the main trolling line via a sliding snap about halfway between the planer board and the boat. Where legal, sliders cover a wider swath of water and with a variety of baits to pinpoint what walleyes want on a given day. Use a heavier dropper line than your main line to help prevent tangling. The key is to vary the depth (by adding more weight or longer line) and spinners and crankbaits until you start getting hit.

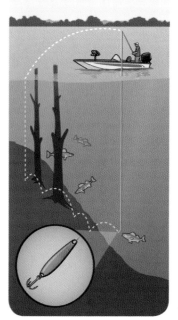

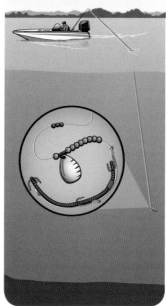

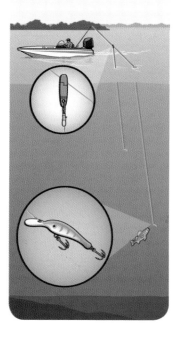

LIGHTEN UP A Roach rig is a classic setup for slowly trolling or drifting bait along bottom structure that employs a special walking stinger; it's a great tactic when the bite turns tough. Lighten things with a 6-pound (2.7 kg) mono main line, a ⅜-ounce (11 g) sinker, and a 4- to 8-foot-long (1.2 to 2.4 m) 4-pound (1.8 kg) leader. Anchor above marked fish and present rig vertically. With your finger on the line, you'll feel the minnow get livelier when a walleye is on its tail. That's when you open the bail to let the bait swim free.

CRANK A CRAWLER The crawler harness isn't just for bottom fishing anymore. When walleyes suspend high in the water column (where multiple lines are legal), pair this traditional favorite with a deep-diving crankbait. Here's how to rig it: A 3-way swivel goes on the end of your main line. To the top ring, tie a 5-foot (1.5 m) leader and connect a crawler harness with a quick-change clevis. On the remaining ring, tie a 10-foot (3 m) leader and attach a snap and crankbait to change baits easily until you hit gold.

BE A JERK Aggressive postspawn walleyes are just as quick as bass to clobber what appears to them to be a wounded baitfish. Take advantage of this tendency by casting longer jerkbaits to shorelines, rockpiles, or submerged weeds in 2 to 6 feet (.6 to 1.8 m) of water. Point rod tip toward the water and be sure to snap it sharply back three or four times while reeling in slowly to create an erratic, rolling action. Pause several seconds and resume snapping. Be ready for walleyes to strike on the pause.

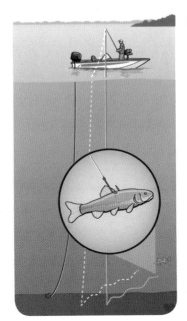

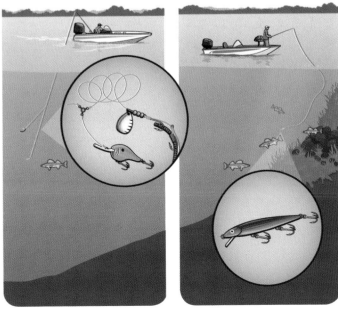

137 GET A BIG YELLOW

As the water warms, yellow perch will move deeper to gravelly areas, where they're easier to spot on sonar.

When angling for big perch, opt for a walleye-size jig. The 1/8-ounce (3.5 g) size is a workhorse, but you may go as heavy as 3/8 ounce (10.6 g) in windy conditions. Dress jig with a minnow and tip hook with a 2- to 3-inch (5 to 8 cm) shiner or fathead. Key on rocky points and reefs in the lake's main basin, particularly the edges where the boulders transition to gravel.

Jumbo perch hug the boulder-strewn bottom when feeding 8 to 12 feet (2.4 to 3.6 m) deep in early June, which makes them hard to see on a depthfinder. Find them by trolling jigs with an electric motor, pulling slowly enough to keep the lines nearly vertical. After locating jumbos, anchor and make short casts. Long throws will result in frequent snags.

Big perch go deeper as water warms, but jumbos don't hold as tight to the bottom as their smaller brethren do. To take advantage of this, anchor over the perch and drop a jig straight to the bottom. Snap jig up a foot (30 cm) and let it hang just above bottom for 10 to 15 seconds before the next snap. Try a medium-to-light-action 7½-foot (2.2 m) spinning rod matched with a limber 6-pound (2.7 kg) monofilament.

138 CATCH NIGHTTIME SMALLMOUTHS

The biggest smallmouths in any lake head for the shoreline as soon as the sun sets because crayfish that have been hiding all day begin to stir, and the bass can grab an easy meal. Start by mounting black lights on the sides of your boat. These crazy purple bulbs aren't just for disco parties; they also illuminate only the first 30 to 50 feet (9 to 12 m) of water from the point where they're mounted and light up fluorescent lines without spooking fish.

Quietly motor in on rocky banks and points, staying 70 to 90 (21 to 27 m) feet away, and then flick on the black lights. Use a 14-pound (6 kg) fluorescent monofilament with a 4-inch (10 cm) crawdad in black or blue up against the bank on a Texas rig. The retrieve at night is no different from doing it by day, but the lights make everything glow in the dark. As soon as you see the line move, you set.

Some people believe that night fishing with a black light and fluorescent line will actually make any angler a better daytime soft-plastic fisherman because the nighttime system makes the take so visual.

139 KNOW YOUR BROOK TROUT

Technically a member of the char family, "brookies" are the only trout native to the northeastern United States, with their natural range extending from the Appalachian Mountains from Maine to Georgia. Today native brook trout populations suffer due to global warming and development throughout their range. Still, cults of anglers in the Northeast hunt the tiny natives on light fly and spinning tackle in hidden streams that flow clear and cold. Natural brook trout are hard to find, but this fish is raised in hatcheries throughout the country and makes up a number of stocked fish that end up in waterways every spring and fall. Whether they're native or hatchery-raised, count on them being aggressive; brook trout often take a swipe at almost any lure or fly that gets in front of their face.

140 FIND TROUT IN THE DARK

Bushy streamers that splash and gurgle are the typical nighttime flies of choice for trout fishermen. For something different, when you have the best pools to yourself on a quiet night, try catching big browns and rainbows on dry flies. At night, color doesn't mean anything. It's all about silhouette. Tie on a slightly larger size than you'd use during the day, with a white wing for visibility. Anchor in a slow pool just before dark. Once your eyes adjust, you'll be able to pick out rises.

Unlike in a daytime approach, don't try to lead

a trout at night. When you see a dimple on the surface, cast right to that spot. To make it easier, target fish rising 30 feet (9 m) away or less and go fishing on nights with plenty of moonlight. You might not know exactly where your fly is, but the goal is to land as close to the rise as possible. In the dark, it's difficult to determine whether you overshot or undershot the fish. If you lay out and see the dimple again, just lift the rod instead of setting. Either the fish will be on or it won't. If it's not, you just lay out again to the same spot.

KNOW YOUR CARP

Common carp, mirror carp, and grass carp are all invasive species, brought to the United States from Europe and Asia and released in American waters. They have flourished. Carp are hardy and adapt to warm and cold climates; they can be found in almost every state. It wasn't long ago when many U.S. anglers considered carp a "trash fish." That's changed recently, thanks to an interest in methods adopted from Europe, where carp fishing has always been popular, and the discovery that carp can be caught on the fly. Today major U.S. fly tackle manufacturers offer rods, flies, and line just for carp. They're big—often hitting the 50-pound (22 kg) range—giving fly guys a much harder fight than the average trout. They're omnivores, so they'll eat a berry fly on the surface or a crawfish fly stripped along the bottom. For the non-fly angler, European bite alarms, boilie baits, and other carp tackle are becoming more available.

142 FLATLINE FOR CRAPPIES

In this least complicated kayak trolling method, the line is attached to a lure without any secondary weight or device added. Usually a near-surface technique, flatlining reaches moderate depths by trolling jigs or diving crankbaits. Crappies are common targets for summer flatline trollers. In many lakes, crappie schools suspend 10 to 15 feet (3 to 4.5 m) deep, sometimes near structure but just as often in open waters. Here's the tactic:

Spool 4- or 6-pound (1.8 or 2.7 kg) monofilament on common midweight spinning outfits. Crappies are soft-mouthed; a flexible rod tip keeps hooks from tearing out. Two-inch-long (5 cm), $\frac{1}{16}$- and $\frac{1}{8}$-ounce (1.7 to 3.5 g) crappie jigs are used most commonly with this technique. If you troll with two or more rods, rig with jigs of differing weights or colors.

Slow-troll at 1 mph (best measured using a GPS unit) with one jig 30 feet (9 m) behind the boat and another jig 60 feet (18 m) back. The more line you have out, the deeper a jig will run. This jig can be as deep as 10 or 12 feet (3 to 3.6 m), depending also on weight. Experiment with line length, jig size, and color. Throw out a marker buoy as a target for your next trolling pass and then match your other trolling rod to the line length and jig that took the first fish.

For flatline trolling with diving plugs, fine-diameter superline gives you up to 20 percent greater trolling depth compared to 10-pound (4.5 kg) nylon monofilament, as thinner superlines have less water resistance. You'll get better hooksets, too, because superlines have less stretch.

143 ADJUST THE CONTRAST

In the summer, bass pros say, you have a much better chance at a true hog of a largemouth after dark. Boat traffic in the day makes a lot of noise and it's hard for bass to pick up on the sound of natural bait. They may strike during the day because they're confused by the engine noise, but once they make mistakes a few times, they'll just stop feeding when it's light.

Instead, wary bass go on the hunt when the water quiets down at night. To catch them, patrol flats with quick access to deeper water, where the fish will move in to feed. Use a ¾-ounce (7 g) short-arm spinner-bait with a single Colorado blade. The heavy lure sinks quickly, which is key to using a pump-and-stop retrieve that will mimic a crayfish hopping along the bottom. At night, contrast is more important than color.

Use a black or purple spinnerbait with a white pork-chunk trailer. The trailer creates a difference in contrast. Big bass usually hit anything moving the right way that stands out a little.

144 SEE A CAT IN THE DARK

Hooking a 60-pound (27 kg) flathead in the dark is all about working the fish out of the submerged tree where you likely found it. To win this tree-hopping night game, you'll want both a specialized rig and an application of brute force.

Live bluegills are great bait, but you don't want them swimming around, tangling in the trees. So instead of a single hook and leader, rig the bait on a 1-ounce (28 g) jighead, passing the hook through the bottom jaw and out one eye. The jighead is tied to a 30-pound (14 kg) mono main line.

Using a 7-foot (2 m) heavy-action conventional rod, drop the bait straight down, working all around a submerged tree, starting on the deep side and moving to the shallow side. The heavy jighead provides better contact with and control of the bluegill in the sticky stuff. As cats may be on the bottom or suspended among limbs, it's important to work the entire water column.

Each drop should last only about 20 seconds. Give the bait a twitch or two then move on. If the fish is there, it'll bite pretty fast.

145

POWER UP

Power plants are often built along rivers so they can draw necessary cooling water. Heated water flows out into the river, drawing bait and gamefish like a magnet in winter. If the area is legally accessible, look for fish in these spots.

MOUTH Large predators, such as muskies and striped bass, will patrol the area where warm discharge water meets cold river water (A). They're less interested in small bait, so work a perch-color twitchbait near the end of the chute or live-line big baits like suckers or shad.

BANK Walleyes and large smallmouths tend to hang along the sides of the discharge chute out of the main current (B), waiting for forage to flush down to them. Hop a white grub on a jighead through the water below any current break.

HEAD Baitfish congregate near the head of the discharge, where the water is the warmest (C). Crappies, perch, and smallmouths hang in the calmer water next to the center flow, picking off bait that washes into the eddy.

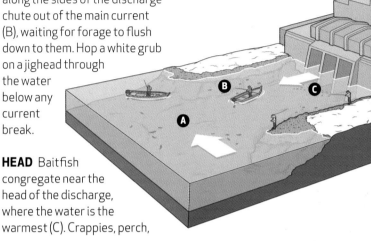

146

KNOW YOUR CHINOOK SALMON

Also known as king salmon, this is the largest member of the salmon family and can weigh more than 90 pounds (40 kg). Native to the Pacific Coast from Northern California to Alaska, Chinooks are prized for their quality on the table and their brute fighting ability. In late spring through early summer (and in fall in the case of Great Lakes salmon), Chinooks return to the rivers of their birth from the ocean, where saltwater anglers wait to intercept them in bays with trolling spoons and jigs, and fly and conventional anglers line rivers to throw plugs and streamers as the fish migrate upstream. Once salmon enter rivers to spawn, they stop feeding. Striking at a lure or fly is purely an aggressive reaction. Popular salmon lure and fly colors are rarely natural but instead bright and flashy to essentially annoy a salmon into biting.

147 CHERRY-PICK THE TREES

Trying to find reservoir largemouths from midsummer through September, when bass follow schools of baitfish moving unpredictably around the lake, can be maddening. Experienced anglers will tell you that this can all change once you know these two basic things (1) The fish usually suspend 8 to 12 feet (2.4 to 3.6 m) deep over much deeper water; and (2) isolated clumps of flooded timber near dropoffs and points serve as rest stops and snack stations for these roving bass. Work such trees at the right depth, and you'll consistently catch heavyweights when nobody else can find the fish. Use these tips for greater success.

CHECK THE CONIFERS The maze of branches (A) that extend from cedar and pine trees give bass a dense sanctuary. Fish tend to cling to the odd type of cover in a given area, so look for a cedar surrounded by hardwoods.

DROP THE RIGHT PLASTIC Once you identify your target spot, cast a 10-inch (25 cm) worm rigged with a 4/0 hook and a 3/16-ounce (5 g) bullet sinker to the center of the limbs (B) with a medium-heavy baitcasting outfit matched with 15- to 20-pound (7 to 9 kg) monofilament.

FALL FOR IT Count the worm down about 10 feet (3 m) on a semi-slack line. Most strikes are going to come on the initial drop. If not, hop and swim the worm back through the limbs (C).

HARDWOODS The upper branches of many hard-woods (D) spread out and offer bass numerous hiding places. Trees with more horizontal limbs generally attract more bass than trees with vertical ones. The thickest limbs tend to hold the biggest bass.

BUSTING BRUSH Flip a 1/2-ounce (14 g) jig-and-pig to the trunk of a cedar tree with a stiff flipping rod and 25-pound (11 kg) monofilament or 50-pound (23 kg) braided line. Let the line drape over a branch and work the jig down, a few feet at a time (E), to a depth of 10 to 12 feet (3 to 3.6 m). Jig the bait up and down at each level to coax strikes. When a bass nabs the lure, set the hook with all your strength and horse it out before the fish can wrap the line.

THE SHADE FACTOR Fishing standing trees is best when the sun shines. The light drives bass into shade beneath the branches (F). Cast to the shaded sides of trees and limbs to get strikes.

WHERE TO LOOK Search for trees poking just above the surface in water 20 feet (6 m) or deeper on main-lake areas and in the lower third of major creek arms. The most productive are located on the ends of points, near creek-channel bends and on the edges of deep flats and dropoffs.

WHAT TO LOOK FOR Sometimes a small limb that sticks a few inches above the surface is the tip-off to an overlooked tree. Wear polarized sunglasses to help spot underwater timber.

148 BEAT THE DRAW-DOWN

Reservoirs release water to draw-down high levels at the same time crappies are moving into postspawn patterns. This creates a challenge: Fish could be 4 feet (1.2 m) deep in 20 feet (6 m) of water, or 10 feet (3 m) deep in 10 feet (3 m) of water. Here's how to search for slabs.

PRESENTATION Slow troll along breaklines, riprap, and points (A). Try using a jig, and go slowly enough that lines drop straight down. The fish are moving to colder water, following the baitfish, which you'll often find in faster moving currents. Use a fishfinder to locate baitfish. To maximize results, fish two rods, each rigged with different jigs, at different depths.

TACKLE Try a longer rod (10 feet [3 m]) and a baitcasting reel (B). Extra length delivers more hooksetting power and keeps lures away from the boat to cover more water. Use a reel with a brake that lets you place baits precisely in tight cover.

Go with 8- to 10-pound (3.6 to 4.5 kg) test line for enhanced strike detection.

LURES Rig two jigs per rod, spacing them about 18 inches (45 cm) apart (C). Tie the first with a Palomar knot, leaving a 2-foot-long (60 cm) tag end to which you fasten the second with another Palomar. Adjust jig depth until you get into fish. In calm conditions, use 1/8-ounce (3.5 g) jigs top and bottom. In strong wind or current, use a 1/4-ounce (7 g) jig as the lower lure.

149 REIGN IN THE RAIN

If bass refuse to belt your spinnerbait during a rain shower, they may be guarding beds and unwilling to chase the lure. While it's harder to see the beds through a rain-rippled surface, the bass also have trouble seeing you, which makes them less inclined to spook and more likely to bite. Take advantage of this by pitching a 3½-inch, (9 cm) tube into beds. One favored color combo is chip gold (flake) and watermelon, rigged Texas-style with a 3/0 offset hook, a 3/16-ounce (5.3 g) bullet sinker, and 17-pound (8 kg) line. The heavy line will wrestle bass out of beds nestled in nasty cover.

150 COVER THE COVER

Largemouths will charge spinnerbaits from any type of cover, but they tend to show a preference for various areas on any given day. Find out where the bass are currently holding and then focus your efforts accordingly. You need to probe shallow grassbeds, boat docks, stumps, flooded bushes, the limbs of fallen trees, and any other available cover until the bass tell you where to fish for them.

Take advantage of your lure's characteristics when searching for these bass. The spinnerbait is one of the most snag-resistant lures and efficiently combs vast amounts of water (even at low speeds). Cast beyond the cover when possible and then guide your spinnerbait close to it with your rod tip. Don't overlook riprap and rocky banks; bass often position themselves nearby in shallow water when it rains. Move your boat close to the bank, cast parallel to the shoreline, and keep your bait hard to the rocks throughout the retrieve. When a bass takes a shot, you'll know, because it won't be subtle.

151 GO SLINGIN' IN THE RAIN

A spinnerbait is my first choice for wet springtime bass fishing. Rain usually means a falling barometer, which makes bass more inclined to feed and chase. The dark skies and dimpled surface reduce light penetration and encourage bass to move to the edges of their cover, for a much-enlarged strike zone. You don't have to put your bait within inches of a bass's nose to prompt a bite. Merely get it close enough for the fish to see it or sense the vibration through its lateral lines. A bass in rainy-day mode won't overlook a flashing spinnerbait. To fish shallow water in steady rain, I like to use a light-colored lure, usually a white 3/8- or 1/2-ounce (11 to 14 g) to spinnerbait with nickel blades. I opt for rounded Indiana or Colorado blades, which have more lift, when I want to run the lure slowly just beneath the surface. If I need to retrieve the bait a little faster or deeper, I switch to narrower willowleaf blades. Heavy 15- to 20-pound (7 to 9 kg) test line helps reduce break-offs in thick cover. When the rain breaks, I downsize. A big spinnerbait fished in slick water may look too gaudy to bass. I've had success going as small as 1/8 ounce (3.5 g), in white, with a No. 2 Indiana and a No. 3 Colorado or Oklahoma blade. If you can't find a small spinnerbait in one of these combinations, buy one that has a Colorado lead blade and a willowleaf trailing, and replace the latter with another Colorado. I fish these versions just as I do the larger ones, and with the same heavy line—and I draw strikes from sizable bass.

152 GIVE IN TO BLIND AMBITION

Ice and snow can make figuring out where to fish on a new lake or pond challenging. First, you need a depth chart. Look for areas that match with the species you're targeting. For warmwater fish like bass and pike, look for weedy areas. For trout or salmon, dropoffs are productive. For all species, look for offshore humps. Mark these on the map, then set tip-ups in the strike zone.

STEP 1 Drill 11 holes in a U-pattern across gradients. Set two rows of tip-ups—starting about 40 yards (37 m) apart—at 5, 10, 15, 20 (1.5, 3, 4.5, and 6 m), and 25 feet (7.5 m) deep. Set the last tip-up in 30 feet (9 m) of water between the two rows. If there is an offshore hump in the area, set a couple more tip-ups there at 5 and 10 feet (1.5 and 3 m). This spread puts bait in front of fish traveling along gradients and hunting in the area.

STEP 2 Rig the shallower tip-ups, those at 5 and 10 feet (1.5 and 3 m) (and the hump set), with

the biggest baits, like a shiner, because the fish at these depths will be hunting. The deeper sets get smaller baits, as these fish may be less active. Drill additional holes by the hump and the deepest sets where you and your buddy can work jigs. You'll put a few panfish in your bucket and draw the attention of a bigger predator fish. If nothing else, the activity will help keep you warm as you wait for a bite.

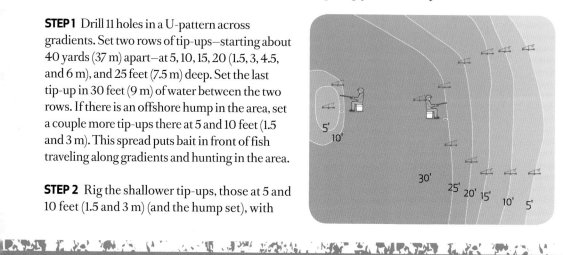

153 KNOW WHEN YOU'RE ON THIN ICE

Ice is generally said to be thick enough for walking and fishing at 4 inches (10 cm), but not all ice is created equal. Clear ice that forms in December will be stronger than the same depth in March, when the bonds fusing the crystals have become stressed from spring sunlight, giving it a honeycomb appearance. Color counts. Beware of black, gray, or milky ice, which lacks the strength of clear green or blue ice. Snowpack or standing water weakens ice. Steer clear of rocks and logs, which can conduct heat to the surrounding ice. Decaying vegetation leads to unstable conditions.

Ice near shore will be weaker than ice that forms over open water. Springs and inlets can prevent the formation of safe ice. Even waterfowl and fish slow ice formation by circulating water.

The golden rule is "Probe as you go." Use an ice chisel or spud bar with a sharpened point. Safe ice sounds solid and dull when thumped. Rotting ice creaks or feels spongy. A single hard jab will usually break through ice less than 3 inches (8 cm) thick. If in doubt, test with an auger or cordless 1/4-inch (6 mm) drill with a 5/8-inch (16 mm) wood auger bit. Carry a tape measure for precise measurement.

154 JIG BIG LAKERS IN SKINNY WATER

Ice fishing has its own special set of challenge, and its own set of awesome rewards. The challenges? Well, let's just say that fighting a jumbo lake trout through a hole in the ice is an intense experience, but to get that massive beast weighing 20 pounds (9 kg) or more on the line, you have to think outside the box when hunting on the hard water. One pro tip is to skip the deep water and go shallow. Legendary Colorado ice guide Bernie Keefe frequently jigs in as little as 3 feet (1 m) of water, provided there is deeper water close by. Keefe tells his clients that big lakers in deep water can more often than not be finicky. That said, if a monster comes in shallow, it's there for one reason only—a fast meal. You won't have light taps and half-hearted strikes. A laker on shallow flats wants to grab a meal and get back to the nearby depths fast, so your jig won't just get hit—it'll get slammed. Hang on tight.

155

BE A WALLEYE PUPPET MASTER

Swimming jigs are to walleyes what jelly donuts are to bears, but surprisingly few ice fishermen use them. The lure itself is nothing new, but a little puppet mastery will bring the jig to life. Here are the most effective motions:

LIFT AND DROP Try this basic action framed within the first 2 feet (60 cm) off the bottom. Use some finesse here—a light, smooth snap fares better than a sudden jerk. Add a circular motion to give the lure an erratic movement, which the walleye interprets as a bait in distress—in other words, dinner. Walleyes typically hit the lure on the drop. Subsequently, the next lift develops into a hookset.

SHIMMY AND SWIM Walleyes are known to be stingy biters. When that happens, reduce the range to 6 inches (15 cm) and soften the stroke. On a taut string, the lure continues making deliciously unpredictable moves, but without the octane. Do a shimmy—basically an in-place quiver—every half-dozen lifts. That kind of nervous behavior can propel a wary walleye to bite.

Try these tricks on a medium-action 28- to 30-inch (71 to 76 cm) rod and 10-pound (4.5 kg) braided line for improved feel, with a 2- to 4-foot-long (.6 to 1.2 m) 8-pound (4 kg) test monofilament shock leader. The inherent stretch of mono line helps set the hook without pulling the lure from the walleye's mouth.

156 DRILL DOWN ON IT

When fishing from a boat, most anglers move around the lake and try new spots all day, but in ice fishing, many just drill holes over spots that have been productive in the past and stay put. The thing is, making the effort to move on the ice and drill lots of holes will get you more fish. Since you can't cast in different directions on the ice to run your lure through new pieces of water, drilling holes even 20 feet (6 m) apart can increase hookups significantly, especially when fishing species like lake trout, pike, and walleyes that tend to roam around an area. There could be fish all around your lure or bait that just don't get close enough to see it, but a redrill a short distance away will put the offering right in the zone. Some ice fishing guides will drill more than 100 holes a day and cover 3 miles (5 km) of lake, and they usually catch the most fish. I also landed the biggest lake trout I've ever caught through the ice after three drops into a hole not 30 feet (9 m) from one I'd been jigging for an hour.

157 CATCH A SHAD-MAD CAT

Pike nuts know all about the bite that coincides with ice-out. But what few anglers know is that an abundance of bait—winter-killed shad—makes this one of the best times of the year to catch catfish. Just be sure to dress warmly. As an outfit for these ice-cats, try an 8-foot, 6-inch (2.5 m) steelhead rod, matched with a reliable baitcaster with a good drag. Spool the reel with 10-pound (4.5 kg) monofilament.

Shallow, dark-bottomed still water—1 to 3 feet (30 to 90 cm) deep—adjacent to deeper current channels warms earliest. Dead shad collect in the eddies, and catfish cruise over a wide area, taking advantage of the bounty. So many dead shad are on the bottom that the cats are cherry-picking the choicest morsels, the innards. Look for floaters along the bank or gather live bait with a cast net. Put a 3/8-ounce (11 g) barrel sinker, 5 mm glass bead, and snap-swivel on the end of your line. Finish the rig with an 18-inch (46 cm) braided leader and No. 1 red baitholder hook. String the guts on the hook as you would a big nightcrawler, and squirt artificial shad scent on the guts every time you recast.

158 GET A JUMP ON STEALTHY SNOOK

A guide once told me that a snook is like a mugger in an alley—it hides in the shadows, waiting for prey to pass by. Then it bolts out and attacks. Snook are nocturnal feeders, and many guides base a hunt around tidal flow. These fish prefer to let the tide bring a meal to them, and they'll use any structure that breaks the current—particularly dock pilings and bulkheads—as ambush points. A high outgoing tide is best; a slack tide hardly ever produces fish. If you find a lighted dock that creates a strong shadow in the water, you've hit big-snook

pay dirt, but fooling a fish hiding under the boards boils down to proper presentation. Never pitch a bait directly to the spot the snook is likely holding in. Cast uptide and let the bait naturally move down into the light. If it doesn't get attacked in three or four casts, either the fish isn't there or it's not going to eat.

Opt for a live pinfish or finger mullet pinned through the nose with a 4/0 circle hook and rigged weightless on a 30-inch (76 cm) length of 40-pound (18 kg) fluorocarbon. The heavy leader will withstand abrasion

on pilings and on a snook's sharp gill plate. When a snook does grab the bait, it's critical to fight it with the rod first and the reel second because low severe rod angles are often necessary to get the fish away from the structure.

159 KNOW YOUR RED DRUM

Also known as redfish, this inshore saltwater species is one of the most widely distributed in the country. What makes these fish so popular is that you can adapt almost any fishing style to their pursuit. Flyfishermen can delicately present crab flies to tailing reds in shallow coastal marshes of the Florida Everglades. Surf-casters working the rough shores of North Carolina can fire chunks of fresh menhaden in hopes of scoring a giant "bull" red from the sand. Anglers working the dirty water at the mouth of the Mississippi River in Louisiana will get drags screaming by working a popping cork and soft-plastic shrimp. No matter where or how you hook a red, be ready for a fight. Big fish weighing 20 to 50 (9 to 23 kg) pounds will drain a spool of line and dog to the bitter end.

160

FIND STRIPERS IN THE DARK

Summer success with nighttime stripers often means moving away from the main beach and targeting areas with current where nonmigratory bass stake claims during the hot months. Inlets—especially those with bridges—are good spots, as a falling tide will draw forage from the bay to the bass stationed near the inlet mouth or behind pilings.

If you can learn how to swing a plug, you'll catch a lot more bass than you would just by reeling. To do this, try casting upcurrent at a 45-degree angle, then lock the reel and never turn the handle. As the line comes tight in the current, the lure will dig and start swimming across the current on its own. To a bass, this scene looks like a dead floating

baitfish that suddenly came to life. It's a real strike trigger.

Even after the line straightens out, you'll want to give the lure at least 20 seconds of extra hang time to entice any reluctant bass

before retrieving for another cast. The trick after catching one fish is to repeat the same swing again and again, as stripers will often congregate in a small area.

161 POP ON OVER

Many saltwater anglers are married to the idea that if they don't see any gamefish feeding on the surface, there's no use in casting a topwater lure. But that's actually the opposite of the truth. Sometimes when the ocean just seems completely devoid of life and you can't get bit no matter what lures or jigs you try below the surface, a topwater lure can draw a strike, even from a fish holding at a considerable depth. Why? Because sound is powerful, and sometimes the chugging and splashing of a popper on an otherwise quiet surface is the little trigger that gets lockjawed fish chewing. Next time you're marking fish on your sounder but can't get them to eat, make a handful of casts with a loud popper or Spook-style lure with rattles. The monster striper, snook, redfish, or seatrout that rises to the occasion might shock you.

ATTRACTOR FLY A large flashy dry fly designed to grab a trout's attention; does not mimic a specific insect.

BACK CAST Any point during fly casting when the line is in the air behind you.

BACKLASH When the line on the spool of a reel tangles or knots, usually caused by loose line on the spool, wind, or the spool revolving too quickly on the cast.

BANK SINKER A rounded weight designed to roll and move across the bottom instead of anchoring a rig or bait.

BEADHEAD A small brass or tungsten head used to add extra flash and weight to nymph and streamer flies.

BEDDED Refers to any fish that's positioned over or guarding a nest of eggs.

BELLY BOAT A tube with shoulder straps and a seat harness that allows an angler to float in a body of water; fins are worn on the feet to allow the angler to maneuver.

BOBBER STOP A knot of string or rubber bead threaded on the line that stops a slip bobber from sliding up the line. Placement of a bobber stop determines how deep the bait or jig below can sink before it suspends below the float.

BOTTOM BOUNCER A weight with a long wire arm that ticks along the bottom while drifting. The arm helps keep the weight from hanging in rocky bottoms.

BRAIDED LINE Any fishing line woven from strands or fibers of materials such as Dyneema, Dacron, or Spectra. Typically thinner and stronger than monofilament.

BUCKTAIL JIG A lure with a weighted lead head and a tail made from the hair of a deer's tail.

BULLET WEIGHT A bullet-shape sliding sinker most often used to rig soft-plastic lures Texas or Carolina style.

BUTT The last section of a fishing rod, located behind the reel seat.

BUZZBAIT A skirted topwater lure with a wire arm that features a plastic propeller on the end. When retrieved, the propeller creates noise and a bubble trail on the surface.

CADDIS A classification of water-borne insects that consists of over 12,000 species found in rivers, streams, ponds, and lakes throughout the U.S. Many fly styles mimic caddis in various stages of their life cycle.

CANE POLE A fishing rod made from bamboo. There is no reel, but rather a fixed length of line tied to the end.

CAROLINA RIG A rig with a bullet weight slid up the main line, followed by a glass bead. A barrel swivel is then tied to the end of the main line to stop the weight and bead from sliding any lower. A leader is tied to the other end of the barrel swivel, and the hook that will hold the soft-plastic lure is tied to the opposite end of the leader. The bead and weight will bang together to make a clicking sound.

CIRCLE HOOK A round hook that is designed specifically to catch in the corner of a fish's mouth. Circle hooks are supposed to thwart gut hookings, thus improving the odds of healthy releases. These hooks are favored by anglers who chase large species that require giving the fish time to run off with the bait.

CLEVIS A piece of terminal tackle that holds a spinner blade to the wire arm of an in-line spinner or spinnerbait. The clevis rotates around the arm, giving the blade its action. Some clevises are designed to allow anglers to quickly change blade colors and styles.

CONEHEAD WEIGHT A conical metal head used to add weight to streamer flies.

CRANKBAIT A family of lures usually made of hard plastic that produce a tight wobble when reeled with a steady retrieve. Most crankbaits have lips that determine how deep they dive, though some lipless versions exist. Crankbaits are typically used to mimic baitfish or crayfish.

CREATURE Soft-plastic lures that do not mimic a particular species of forage, but rather incorporate unnatural tentacles, arms, ribs, fins, and claws into their designs to grab the attention of a bass by producing more action, visual stimulation, and vibration than standard soft-plastic styles.

CUTBANK A bank of a river or stream that's been gouged out by the current, creating an indented pocket underwater and an overhanging lip above the water.

DEAD DRIFT This term refers to the drifting of fly down a section of river or stream when the objective is to make the presentation look as natural as possible by not imparting any movement with the rod and controlling your line so the current does not speed up or slow down the fly's drift.

DEADFALL A tangled cluster of dead trees, limbs, or brush in the water.

DEPTHFINDER An electronic device used on boats that measures water depth with sonar.

DORSAL FIN The fin on a fish's back closest to the head.

DOWNRIGGER A device used while trolling to place a lure or bait at the desired depth. It consists of a 3- to 6-foot (1 to 2 m) horizontal pole, which supports a large cannonball weight by a steel cable. A release clip attaches a fishing line to the cannonball weight, which is lowered to the desired depth manually or electronically. When a fish strikes, the line is yanked free of the release clip.

DROPPER RIG A rig used in flyfishing that usually consists of a bulky dry fly and a small nymph. To rig this right, tie a short piece of tippet to the hook of the dry fly, and then tie the nymph to the other end of the tippet. The dry fly keeps the nymph, a.k.a. the "dropper," suspended in the water below it like a bobber during the drift. This allows you to entice fish both on and below the surface simultaneously.

DROP-SHOT RIG A rig used with soft-plastic lures that keeps the lure suspended off the bottom. The hook that holds the lure is usually tied directly to the main line or a loop in the main line, and a 12- to 15-inch (30 to 38 cm) tag end is left below the hook or loop. A special drop-shot weight connects to the bottom of the tag end.

DRY FLY Any bug-imitating fly designed to float or drift on the water's surface.

DUBBING Any material—usually fine hair, fur, or synthetic fibers—used for creating the body of a fly.

EDDY Any point in the flow of moving water where the current moves in the opposite direction of the main current, often creating a small whirlpool or area of calmer slack water. Eddies form most often behind obstructions, such as deadfalls and boulders.

EMERGER This refers to any fly tied to mimic an aquatic insect during the point in its life cycle when it has just hatched off the bottom of a lake or river and is swimming to the surface, where it will dry its wings and fly away.

FALSE CAST Any stroke in fly casting that is made while the line is in the air, and before it is laid down on the water. Used to work line through the guides to extend a cast's length or to build shooting momentum to give a cast more reach.

FISHFINDER An electronic device that uses sonar to draw a digital image of the water column, thereby showing the depth and position of gamefish or baitfish under the boat.

FLASHER An electronic device used to find game- and baitfish through ice. Flashers emit sonar beams, and fish or bait appear as bars of varying thickness on the screen.

FLIP A style of casting used most often in bass fishing to cast jigs or soft-plastic lures to small targets, such as dock pilings or submerged tree stumps only a short distance away from the end of the rod.

FLOATING LINE A fly line engineered to float on the surface, the most commonly used style of fly line.

FLUOROCARBON A material used to make fishing line and leader material that's praised for its abrasion resistance and near invisibility underwater.

FOOTBALL JIG A bass lure with a rubber skirt and a weighted head with an oblong shape.

FREE LINE A live bait presented with no weight on the line, allowing it to swim naturally and freely.

FRENCH-FRY WORM A style of soft-plastic worm, short in length, with a curled body shape.

GAFF A large hook mounted to the end of a pole used to land large fish once they're brought to the side of the boat.

GLIDER A style of muskie and pike lure that darts side to side in long strides underwater when a twitching action is imparted with the rod.

HACKLE Feathers used to create wispy collars or bodies on flies. The term can also refer to the collar of a dry fly.

HATCH Refers to a lot of aquatic insects leaving a body of water after their wings have formed and dried.

GLOSSARY

HOOK HANGER A U-shape eyelet usually found above the reel seat on a rod that offers a place to attach a hook when the rod is not in use.

HYDROLOGICAL MAP Any map that specifically depicts the distribution of water on the Earth's surface.

INDICATOR A small float made specifically for flyfishing that allows the angler to detect strikes when drifting nymphs or wet flies; also called strike indicators.

IN-LINE Any type of lure with a spinner blade that revolves around a single straight wire post.

JERKBAIT A style of lure designed to dart erratically when the rod tip is twitched. Most hard jerkbaits have lips to control how deep they dive with each twitch and longer, more slender bodies than crankbaits. Hard versions of these lures are also called twitchbaits or stickbaits.

JIG Any lure designed to work with a rise-and-fall motion directly below the boat or during the retrieve after casting a distance. Most jigs have a weighted head and tail made from hair, feathers, rubber, or soft-plastic material, though others, such as long, slender metal lures that imitate various baitfish, can also be considered jigs.

JIG-AND-PIG A rubber-skirted lure with a weighted head, coupled with a pork skin or soft-plastic trailer threaded onto the hook to give the lure more action in the water.

JIGHEAD A weight with a hook and eyelet molded directly into lead. Jigheads

come in all shapes and sizes and are most commonly used with soft-plastic lures.

LEADER Any length of mono-filament, fluorocarbon, or wire added by the angler to the end of the main line or fly line for purposes such as bite protection, shock absorption, or reducing the fish's ability to detect the line underwater.

LINDY RIG A bottom rig for live bait presentations that uses a flat sliding sinker that will "walk" over rocky bottoms without getting snagged.

LINE-COUNTER REEL Any reel with a built-in counter that's internally connected to the spool and tells the angler exactly how many feet of line is being let out or reeled in.

LINE-TIE EYE A term used to describe the eye on a lure to which the main line or leader is tied.

LIVIE An angling term that refers to any baitfish that's used in live form.

LOGJAM A group of logs, tree trunks, or limbs that has gotten stuck in a moving body of water and created an obstruction.

LUNKER A slang term that usually refers to a big largemouth bass.

MARKER BUOY Any man-made floating or stationary marker that aids in navigation on the water by denoting the edges of a channel, a shipping lane, the entrance to a harbor, or an underwater obstruction.

MAYFLY A classification of water-borne insects with very short life spans.

Mayflies found in rivers, streams, ponds, and lakes throughout the U.S. are common trout forage in both larval and adult form. Many fly styles mimic mayflies in various stages of their life cycle.

MEND To lift any fly line between the rod tip and the fly off the water after the cast and place it upstream so the fly always precedes the line during a drift. Mending allows a wet fly or nymph to sink deeper, and when you dry fly fish, mending helps attain a drag-free drift.

MONOFILAMENT Fishing line made from a single fiber of polymers that have been melted and extruded through holes of varying sizes that determine line thickness and breaking strength.

NOODLING The act of using your hands and feet as catfish bait by sticking them in underwater holes and rockpiles, wiggling them, allowing the catfish to clamp down, and wrestling it out of the hole.

NYMPH Any fly designed to fish below the surface that mimics an aquatic insect in the post-larval, but pre-adult, stage of its life cycle. In biology, nymph is also the general term for aquatic insects in their pre-adult life cycle stage.

PARTY BOAT Fishing vessels open to the public that can accommodate a large group of anglers. Most of the time, no prior reservations are needed, as anglers can simply walk onto the boat and pay the fare onboard. Mainly found near oceans and on big lakes.

PLANER BOARD Used for trolling, planer boards are made from plastic or wood and have a beveled edge. Some planer boards are pulled with special rods separate from the rod pulling bait or lure or on thin ropes, and fishing line attaches to the board via a tension release clip. Some lighter planer boards are attached directly to the main line and do not snap free after a strike. Both styles pull the line off to one side of the boat when deployed, widening trolling spread and allowing anglers to fish more lines by keeping them separated.

PLUG Any long hardbait with a diving lip that mimics large baitfish species, such as herring, suckers, or menhaden. Technically, there is no difference between a plug and a large, long crankbait, but the term is commonly used in saltwater fishing and by pike and muskie anglers.

POPPER Any topwater lure with a cupped mouth designed to chug and spit, and to spray water as it's moved across the surface.

QUICK-STRIKE RIG A live-bait rig used in muskie fishing. It features two treble hooks connected with wire leader, one of which is placed in a baitfish's head and the other in the tail so a hook ends up in a muskie's mouth no matter which end of the bait it attacks. Only one point of each treble hook is placed in the bait so upon the hookset, the hooks pull free of the bait quickly and stick in the muskie's hard mouth.

RATTLEBAIT A term used to refer to a lipless crankbait with internal rattles.

REEL RATIO A fraction that defines how many inches or feet (centimeters or meters) of line are wound onto a reel spool with each revolution of the handle.

RIFFLE A choppy section of a river or stream caused by the water moving over a shallow rock-strewn area, sandbar, or gravel bar.

RIPRAP A term that refers to man-made underwater structure, such as old building foundations, old docks, or piles of concrete blocks.

SABIKI RIG A rig that's commonly used for catching baitfish species such as herring that features 6 to 10 tiny feathered hooks on one leader with a weight on the bottom. Sabiki rigs mimic an entire school of very tiny baitfish or shrimp and are usually jigged straight up and down below the boat.

SAN JUAN WORM A simple fly pattern that mimics a mealworm or garden worm. These worms are available in a wide variety of colors: brown, pink, and red are top producers.

SEAM Any area in moving water where currents flowing at two different speeds meet as they run parallel to each other, forming a visible border.

SEINE A long net with fine mesh stretched between two stakes that's used to collect baitfish in streams and small ponds.

SHANK The section of a hook between the bend and eye.

SHINER Though there are some species of small fish that are scientifically referred to as shiners, such as the golden shiner, this term has come to refer to any species of small, shiny-scaled baitfish sold in bait shops.

SINK TIP A length of heavy sinking line either added temporarily to the end of a fly line when casting streamers or nymphs to achieve more depth in certain situations, or permanently fused onto the end of a floating fly line for full-time use in deeper water.

SLAB A slang term for a large crappie.

SLINKY WEIGHT A weight cut from a coil of soft lead to form a long cylindrical sinker; also called a pencil weight. Cutting the lead from the coil allows the angler to determine exactly how much weight to use based on water depth and current speed. Most often used in moving water, slinky weights also hang up less frequently on rocky bottoms during the drift.

SLIP BOBBER/SLIP-FLOAT A float that slides freely on the main line or leader and is stopped by a bobber stop. Slip bobbers slide down to the bottom of the line, making it easy to cast. Once they hit the water, the bait or jig sinks and the slip bobber will slide up to the stop, the placement of which determines how deep the jig or bait can sink.

SNAP Terminal tackle tied to the end of a line or leader that acts as a clasp, allowing anglers to quickly change lures or weights without having to cut and retie the line.

SNAP-WEIGHT A weight used in trolling that clips onto the line via a release clip. Snap weights aid in getting lures or bait rigs to the proper trolling depth and are most commonly used in walleye fishing.

SOFT BAIT Any lure made from soft-plastic material.

GLOSSARY

SONAR An electronic system that uses transmitted and reflected underwater sound waves to detect and locate submerged objects or to measure the distance to the floor of a body of water. Depthfinders and fishfinders all use sonar.

SPEY CAST A style of flycasting that is used to cast a fly long distances when there is not enough backcast room behind the angler to execute a traditional overhand cast. Most popular on large rivers where one needs to cover a wide swath of water in one drift. Special rods are made just for this casting style.

SPIDER RIGGING A method of slow-trolling for crappies in which 6 to 10 poles that can measure up to 16 feet (5 m) in length are arranged in an arc around the front of the boat to simultaneously present a lot of baits or small jigs at different depths.

SPINNERBAIT Most often refers to a lure with a weighted head, a rubber skirt, and an L- or V-shape arm extending over the back that holds the spinner blade. Popular because they can be run through thick cover without collecting weeds.

SPLIT RING A formed wire fastener shaped like a circle. Split rings, small versions of the rings commonly used on key chains, are used to attach hooks to eyelets on lures or as a line-tie on a lure.

SPLIT SHOT A small round weight that is crimped directly onto a line or leader. Split shots are available in many sizes, and most are easily opened and closed with your fingers or pliers to allow weight to be added or removed quickly.

SPOOKY Referring to a fish or group of fish that is wary or easily startled by sounds, shadows, or movements.

SPOON A wobbling lure usually made from a single piece of curved metal.

STAGING Refers to the movements of a fish or large group of fish prior to a change of location based on season or spawning time. As an example, crappies stage along deep slopes for a few weeks until water temperature is right to move to the shallows in order to spawn.

STAR-DRAG KNOB The star-shape knob on a conventional reel used to tighten or loosen the drag.

STICKBAIT See *jerkbait*.

STINKBAIT Bait made by grinding natural or synthetic materials into a thick paste, or molding the ground paste into nuggets or chunks. Used in catfishing, stinkbaits are made with foul- or strong-smelling materials, such as garlic, animal blood, or rotten fish. They are supposed to attract catfish by slowly melting underwater and creating a scent trail the fish can follow to the bait.

STONEFLY A classification of water-borne insects that consists of over 3,500 species. Stoneflies are found in rivers, streams, ponds, and lakes throughout the U.S. and they are common trout and bass forage. Many fly variations are tied to mimic stoneflies and, unlike caddis or mayflies, some stoneflies grow quite large.

STREAMER Any fly stripped below the surface to mimic forage that swims, such as baitfish, leeches, or crayfish.

STRIKE INDICATOR See *indicator*.

STRINGER A string or metal chain used to secure fish that will be kept for the table. The stringer can be left in the water while fishing to keep the fish cool and wet. When the trip is over, the stringer allows the angler to drag or carry out the day's catch.

STRIPPING BASKET A shallow rectangular container, similar in shape to a dish-washing tub, worn on a belt at the waist or stomach to hold loose fly line during the cast or retrieve to keep it from getting tangled on the ground or around an angler's feet when wading in still waters.

STRIPPING GUIDE The first and widest guide on a fly rod, designed to allow easier intake of the fly line when stripping a streamer fly or fighting a fish by hand instead of using the reel.

SUCKER A common baitfish species found throughout the U.S. with an underslung mouth that feeds off the bottom using suction. Suckers, most often used live, are used dead for pike and muskies.

SUSPENDING LURE Any lure designed to maintain its position at a certain depth in the water column without sinking any deeper or rising to the surface.

SWIMBAIT A loose classification of hard and soft lures that usually mimic baitfish but differ from standard crankbaits and jerkbaits. Many have a hard plastic head with a diving lip, and a soft-plastic paddle-shape tail that kicks and vibrates during the retrieve. Many anglers use the term to describe a wide variety of soft-plastic shad imitations with molded internal weights and kicking tails.

SWIVEL A piece of terminal tackle that features two eyelets on posts connected at a central barrel-shape or cylindrical hub that allows the eyelets to independently rotate 360 degrees of each other. Swivels, most often used to connect the main line to a length of leader that will hold the hook or lure, reduce line twist by allowing the lure or bait to spin without twisting the main line or leader.

TAILING LOOP When the leader and front section of fly line crashes into rear section of working fly line during a cast, causing knots and tangles and stopping the cast from fully unrolling. Tailing loops occur most often when making casts longer than 50 feet (15 m).

TAILWATER A river whose primary source is water released from the bottom of a reservoir. Tailwater rivers start at the base of dams, and since true tailwaters are formed by water released from the bottom of a reservoir instead of the top, they often maintain consistent temperature year-round.

TANDEM RIG Any rig in fly or conventional fishing that allows the angler to present two baits, lures, or flies at the same time.

TEXAS RIG A method of rigging soft-plastic lures in which a sliding bullet weight is pegged at the node of the soft-plastic, typically rigged weedless style on a wide-gap hook.

THERMOCLINE An abrupt gradient in a large body of still water where layers of water of different temperatures stack on one another without mixing. As warmer water is less dense than cold water, the position of the thermocline can change throughout the season, but will appear on a well-tuned fishfinder or depthfinder as a distinct band in the water column.

TIPPET A length of monofilament or fluorocarbon added to the end of a tapered fly leader to prolong its life by taking away the need to cut down the main leader every time a new fly is tied on. In most cases, the tippet material is the same diameter as the end of the main leader.

TIP-UP A wooden or plastic X-frame with a central post that features a line spool on the bottom of the post, and spring-activated flag on the top of the post. Used in ice fishing, the baited line is lowered into the hole to the desired depth, then the tip-up is positioned over the hole with the spool end of the post in the water. The line is then connected to the spring-activated flag, which remains bent over until a fish strikes, causing the flag to pop up and alert the angler to the bite.

TROLLING The act of imparting action to baits or lures by pulling them through the water behind a boat moving under engine or paddle power.

TROLLING MOTOR A small electric motor usually mounted to the bow of the boat that allows an angler to maneuver around fishing spots or into tight areas quietly and efficiently. Many have a foot pedal to allow the angler to keep casting while the boat is moving.

TROTLINE A long fishing line with many short lines spaced at uniform intervals attached along its length. Each short line has a hook tied to the end that's baited, and the ends of a trotline are usually held in place by two stakes stuck in bottom of a lake or river.

TUBE A style of soft-plastic lure with a hollow bullet-shape body that is shredded into thin strips at the rear to create a tail skirt.

TWITCHBAIT See *jerkbait*.

WACKY RIG A style of rigging soft-plastic worms in which the hook is passed perpendicularly through the center of the bait's body. This style allows the worm to fall horizontally, and sharp twitches of the rod tip produce a fluttering action in which the body quickly flexes into a U shape and straightens again as the lure free falls.

WATER COLUMN Referring to the entire vertical plain of water from the bottom to the surface. If a fish is holding in the middle of the water column, it means it's hovering at a depth roughly halfway between the surface and bottom.

WET FLY Any fly that mimics aquatic insects in their larval or emerger stages that is designed to fish below the surface. True wet flies are unweighted, though many flycasters rope nymphs into the wet fly category. Likewise, flies that imitate salmon eggs or worms could also be considered wet flies.

favorite tricks and techniques and sharing them with

readers. Now go out and catch those fish!

INDEX

INDEX

CREDITS

Waterbury Publications, Inc., Des Moines, IA

Creative Director Ken Carlson
Editorial Director Lisa Kingsley
Associate Design Director Doug Samuelson
Associate Editor Tricia Bergman
Production Designer Mindy Samuelson
Copy Editor Peg Smith
Proofreader Gretchen Kauffman

ABOUT THE AUTHOR

Joe Cermele started his career in outdoor journalism in 2004, covering fishing tournaments for a local magazine in his home state of New Jersey. In 2005, while attending Rider University, he became an intern at *Salt Water Sportsman* magazine, joining the editorial staff full time that same year after graduation. In 2008, he moved to sister publication *Field & Stream*, where he was named Fishing Editor in 2011. His writing appears monthly in the magazine, he blogs weekly on the magazine's website, and also hosts and produces *Field & Stream*'s Hook Shots, an award-winning web-based fishing show with a punk-rock edge. Cermele has fished all over the country and abroad, but when he's not traveling on assignment, you can find him on his boat chasing tuna and striped bass off the Jersey coast, pitching tubes to smallmouth bass on the Delaware River, or flyfishing for trout in New York's Catskill Mountains.

ABOUT THE MAGAZINE

In every issue of *Field & Stream* you'll find a lot of stuff: Beautiful artwork and photography, adventure stories, wild game recipes, humor, reviews, commentary, and more. That mix is what makes the magazine so great and what's helped it remain relevant since 1895. But at the heart of every issue are the skills. The tips that explain how to use the right lure for every situation, the tactics that help you catch that trophy bass, the lessons that you'll pass on to your kids about the joy of fishing—those are the stories that readers have come to expect from *Field & Stream*. You'll find a ton of those skills in *The Essential Fishing Handbook*, but there's not a book big enough to hold them all in one volume. Besides, whether you're new to fishing or an old pro, there's always more to learn. You can continue to expect *Field & Stream* to teach you those essential skills in every issue. Plus, there's all that other stuff in the magazine, too, which is pretty great. To order a subscription, visit www.fieldandstream.com/subscription.